# COOL: THE SIGNS AND MEANINGS OF ADOLESCENCE

The image of restless, apathetic, mopish, awkward teenagers who listen to loud, screeching music, when they are not on the phone, and who insist on dressing, wearing their hair, and behaving exactly like the friends they apparently cannot live without, has become a fixture of the modern social landscape.

During the teenage years, language, dress, musical tastes, and other symbolic systems become the concrete means for identifying with peers. Marcel Danesi calls this period teenagerhood: a socially constructed time-frame that channels the physiological and emotional changes that occur at puberty into patterns of symbolic behaviour. These patterns are then reinforced by the media.

This book represents both a synthesis of Marcel Danesi's research on the semiotics of modern adolescence and his own interpretation of the signficance and implications of our teenage culture. It constitutes a semiotic portrait of the teenager and of the factors that have led to the construction of the teenage persona and culture.

Danesi focuses on the central behavioural trait of teenagerhood – coolness; he defines it and discusses its emergence at or around puberty, and draws up an 'anatomy' of the behaviours associated with it. Danesi discusses the language of teenagers, which he calls 'pubilect,' and concludes with observations on the etiology, evolution, and future course of teenagerhood.

**Marcel Danesi** is professor of Semiotics and Italian Studies, Victoria University, University of Toronto.

MARCEL DANESI

# Cool: The Signs and Meanings of Adolescence

UNIVERSITY OF TORONTO PRESS
Toronto  Buffalo  London

© University of Toronto Press Incorporated 1994
Toronto  Buffalo  London
Printed in Canada

ISBN 0-8020-0467-9 (cloth)
ISBN 0-8020-7483-9 (paper)


∞

Printed on acid-free paper

Toronto Studies in Semiotics
Editors: Marcel Danesi, Umberto Eco, Paul Perron, and
Thomas Sebeok

---

**Canadian Cataloguing in Publication Data**

Danesi, Marcel, 1946–
  Cool : the signs and meanings of adolescence

  (Toronto studies in semiotics)
  Includes bibliographical references and index.
  ISBN 0-8020-0467-9 (bound)  ISBN 0-8020-7483-9 (pbk.)

  1. Teenagers.    I. Title.    II. Series.

  HQ796.D35 1994          305.23′5          C94-931312-2

---

University of Toronto Press acknowledges the financial
assistance to its publishing program of the Canada
Council and the Ontario Arts Council.

This book is dedicated to the memory of my late uncle, Primo Danesi. He made me understand, early in life, that the human spirit manifests itself continuously in actions that are kind and generous.

# Contents

# Preface

Ten years ago, on a warm fall day in early October, I was waiting patiently outside my daughter's school to give her a ride home. I recall vividly to this day how my attention was captivated by an animated conversation that was taking place between two of her female schoolmates. The word *cool* came up continuously and, it seemed to me, strategically throughout the discussion (*He's so cool!*, *Stephanie's really cool, too!*, etc.). My interest as a semiotician and linguist was piqued, and I approached one of the two and asked her rather curtly: 'Excuse me, do you mind telling me what *being cool* means?' It was her answer that stimulated within me an intense desire to investigate and document what it means to be a teenager today. Indeed, immediately thereafter I became virtually obsessed with the idea of studying the behavioural features and manifestations of *coolness* in the contemporary teenager. My daughter's friend answered me matter-of-factly as follows: 'Ya' know, like, uh, it's *cool* to be *cool!*'

That thirteen-year-old's definition of *coolness* simultaneously encapsulates and displays how the teenager thinks and behaves. As a parent suffering, along with my wife, through the agonizing growing pangs of our only offspring, I became both intrigued and alarmed by what I started to find out about teenagers generally. I began to realize rather early in my research that my wife and I were not alone in suffering through daily bouts of exasperation. Restless, apathetic, mopish, awkward youths who listen to loud, screeching music (when they are not on the phone, that is!), who insist on dressing, wearing their hair, and behaving exactly like the friends without whom they cannot seem to live, and who are constantly making their parents' blood boil, are visible throughout the modern social landscape. As I sifted through the data I was collecting on teenage language (Danesi 1988, 1989a), smoking styles (Danesi 1993), and other typical behaviours, I became progressively more interested in delving deeper into the *forma mentis* of the teenager. Today, I have come to the realization that youths have not always been this way, that *teenagerhood* is really a four-decade-old construction of Western society.

Obviously, I am not claiming that troublesome and insubordinate youths have been invented by our age. Indeed, the ancient Greek historian Herodotus tells of a Sumerian letter, dating back 3700 years, in which we can discern an amazingly similar picture of adolescence. This letter (carved in cuneiform on a stone tablet and written by a father) describes a young boy excused by his overindulgent father from working in the fields. Having nothing important to do after school, the idle Sumerian adolescent wandered about the streets, loitered in the public square, sought pleasure, answered his father in an insolent manner, appeared indifferent towards his future, and seemed to have no disposition whatsoever to follow in his father's footsteps. This portrait of a bored and rebellious adolescent from four millennia ago closes the gap of time rather dramatically, seeming all too close to our own age.

But the teenager of today is also unmistakably different. This is because he or she has developed a new social *persona* within a cultural context which allows and encourages its maintenance and evolution. Rock music and various media (magazines, movies, etc.) define and sustain the style, comportment, and mind-set of the modern teenager. The Sumerian adolescent, and young people from all past ages, simply did not live in a social cosmos that made the emergence of this persona virtually inevitable at puberty – a persona that has become so easily recognizable, so *cool!*

Anthropologists have found that in cultures where marriage coincides with the advent of puberty the kinds of behaviours we associate with our own teenagers simply do not emerge. We have, in truth, allowed such behaviours to come into existence by making schooling obligatory and, as a consequence, by prolonging the 'mating period.' Without a high school environment to sustain it, teenagerhood as we now know it would disappear. The high school, with its cliques, dances, parties, and other gregarious activities, provides a unique kind of social universe which sets in motion the crystallization of the teenage persona.

The appearance of certain behavioural traits (facial expressions, discourse styles, dress codes, musical preferences, etc.) on the developmental timetable of children is a sure sign that they have entered a transitional period. The dramatic changes in physical appearance at adolescence, and the emotional changes that accompany them, are traumatic. Teenagers become inordinately concerned about their appearance, believing that everyone is constantly observing them. This is why they talk defensively all the time about how *others* act, behave, and appear. Language, dress, musical tastes, and other symbolic codes become the concrete means for identifying with peers. Indeed, teenagerhood is implanted in a psychosocial time-frame that channels the physiological and emotional changes that occur at puberty into peer-shaped and peer-sanctioned patterns of symbolic behaviour. These patterns are then reinforced in our culture by the media. Teenagers seem to be continually following the lifestyle models that Hollywood and the television networks have intentionally scripted into their adolescent characters.

When teenagers leave the high school environment, they express a sense of loss, coupled, paradoxically, with a sense of relief. No one ever seems to forget their emotion-laden teenage experiences. But, curiously, no one ever regrets having grown out of teenagerhood. Indeed, everyone – teenager, parent, and educator alike – is bound to heave a sigh of relief when teenagerhood, perhaps the most emotionally intense and difficult period in the life cycle of individuals living in modern industrialized cultures, is finally over.

This book represents both a synthesis of my research on the *signs* and *meanings* of modern adolescence and my own interpretation of the significance and implications of our 'teenage culture.' It constitutes a semiotic portrait of the teenager and an analysis of the factors that have led to the crystallization of the teenage persona in our culture. *Semiotics* is a form of scientific inquiry that studies signs and meanings in human thought and behaviour. Signs are the 'substances' we employ to create our artefacts, from words to social institutions. Teenagerhood is anchored within its own peculiar system of signs and meanings.

The opening chapter delineates a history of teenagerhood. I will argue that there is a distinction between *adolescence* and *teenagerhood*. The former is a term that refers to a psychobiologically marked period of human growth and development, whereas the latter refers to the socially induced mind-set that accompanies this period in industrialized cultures. The second and third chapters focus on the central behavioural trait of teenagerhood – *coolness*: the second defines it and discusses its emergence at or around puberty; the third constitutes an 'anatomy' of the behaviours associated with it. The fourth chapter then aims the semiotic spotlight on the language teenagers speak, often called 'slang,' but which I prefer to designate as 'pubilect.' Finally, I will offer, in the fifth chapter, my own observations and reflections on the etiology, evolution, and future course of teenagerhood.

The idea of writing a book on teenagerhood was actually suggested to me by several reporters who heard me speak at public lectures about my research findings. They apparently felt that my findings and insights had a great deal to say to parents, educators, and the public at large. My hope, in fact, is that this book will be read by anyone interested in teenage behaviour or suffering through the teenager-hood of a son or a daughter. So, it is intended not only for semioticians as a documentation of a specific form of social semiosis, but also for parents, educators, and teenagers themselves. It is hoped that my depiction of teenage behaviour in the pages that follow will help the latter to step outside of the symbology that they have acquired through their social ambience, and, perhaps, to come to a better understanding of who they really are. For this reason I have tried to avoid technical jargon or else I have defined any specialized term relating to semiotics.

I wish to thank Sharon Levinsohn, who wrote about my work in the September 1989 issue of the magazine *First for Women*, and Linda Barnard of the *Toronto Sun*, who reported on this work in the 26 January 1991 issue of that newspaper. I must also thank all the research assistants and co-workers who helped me gather data over the years. Luca Ballarini, Anthony Discenza, Stephanie Gonos, Chris De Sousa, and Alan Gordon deserve a special mention. I have also greatly appreciated and benefited significantly by the comments of Paul Colilli of Laurentian University, Floyd Merrell of Purdue University, and Henry Schogt of the University of Toronto, who read the manuscript of this book. Any infelicities that remain are my sole responsibility. I am thankful to Dr Ron Schoeffel of the University of Toronto Press for having encouraged me to write down my ideas in book-length form and for having tolerated the many delays I have caused in getting the manuscript finalized. I would also like to thank Karen Boersma of the University of Toronto Press for her editorial work on the manuscript of this book. Her suggestions have allowed me to improve it considerably. Also to be thanked is Frances Koltowski for her patience and persistence in producing

the camera-ready copy for production by University of
Toronto Press. But my greatest debt of appreciation goes to
my wife, Lucy, and my daughter, Danila. My wife and I
suffered through the agonizing toll that teenagerhood took
on Danila, who, today, has become a source of insight
into the nature and form of this twentieth-century socio-
semiotic phenomenon. They have inspired me to write all
about it.

COOL: THE SIGNS AND MEANINGS
OF ADOLESCENCE

# 1

# A History of Teenagerhood

*At once socially special and specially socialized, '50s teenagers experienced the same things together – through their assigned place in the burgeoning consumer economy, in the increasing uniformity of public school education throughout the states, and in the national media that doted on their idiosyncrasies.*
Doherty (1988: 46)

Although it might seem that teenagers have been around since time immemorial, it turns out that they are, as Doherty (1988: 46) observes, the direct offspring of an incessantly increasing consumerism and a growing dependence upon the media for information and recreation that emerged during the 1950s, changing the course of Western society permanently. It is true, of course, that even the earliest civilizations differentiated between *young* and *old* as biologically and socially significant categories. But the idea of making the pubescent period a specific one for psychologists to study was forged only in 1904, when Stanley G. Hall proposed to his colleagues that they pay more attention to the psychosocial characteristics which marked the developmental phase that began with puberty and ended with adulthood.

It was not until the end of the Second World War that *youths* and *young adults* came to be viewed as distinct *personae* belonging to a new, discrete subculture. The word *persona* requires some elucidation. In ancient Greece, it signified a 'mask' worn by an actor on stage. Subsequently, it came to have the meaning of 'the character of the mask-wearer.' This meaning still exists in the theatre term *dramatis personae* or 'cast of characters' (literally 'the *persons* of the drama'). Eventually, the word came to have its present designation, which is exemplified by the meaning of the English word *person*: namely, any human being considered as a distinct entity. It was the psychoanalyst Carl Jung (1921) who rehabilitated the Greek term *persona* to refer to the individual's 'face to the world'; that is, to the constellation of roles, attitudes, and behaviours by which an individual presents him- or herself to the world in response to social demands. In this book the term *persona* is used in the Jungian sense. It is interesting to note that the connection between 'personhood' and the theatre still remains in our culture. This is why we say that people 'play roles in life,' 'interact,' 'act out their feelings,' 'put on a proper face,' and so on.

The first writer to portray the newly fashioned teenage persona in fiction was J.D. Salinger in his still popular and controversial novel *The Catcher in the Rye*, published in 1951. Shortly thereafter the culturally constructed image of the 'sweet sixteener' was enshrined in books, magazines, songs, television programs, and movies. Songs of the mid and late fifties, with titles like 'Sixteen Candles,' 'Happy Birthday Sweet Sixteen,' and so on, bear witness to the arrival on the scene of a new social persona with a new, recognizable character. By the end of the decade, the sixteenth-birthday party was felt implicitly to signal the end of teenagerhood. It was during this turning-point in North American social history that the term *teenager* gained general currency within the mainstream culture, providing verbal evidence that a new sociological reality had indeed crystallized. The breakpoint of 'sixteen' was extended by a few years during the 'hippie'-influenced sixties and early seventies to encompass the entire high school period.

Today, many of the teen behaviours formed during high school continue way past people's teen years. Cases of 'terminal adolescence,' so to speak, seem to be cropping up with alarming regularity throughout our society!

The extension of the teen years has been carefully nurtured and vigorously reinforced by adult institutions (the market-place, the media, etc.). The social empowerment of the modern adolescent has been brought about by the world of adults. If we sometimes worry about the results, we really have no one to blame but ourselves. The very survival of the current economic structure depends in large part on the conservation of teenagerhood as a social reality. Without it, much of the work related to schooling, to the music and film industries, the clothing business, the fast-food commercial empire – and the list could go on and on – would virtually disappear.

In this opening chapter, I will trace the cultural etiology and history of teenagerhood as I envision it. I will start off by differentiating between *adolescence* and *teenagerhood*. As mentioned, the first literary embodiment of the modern teenager is, in my view, Holden Caulfield, the protagonist of Salinger's *The Catcher in the Rye*. After a brief examination of this early prototype, what follows are historical snapshots of teenagerhood as it evolved from the fifties to the present day. Although it still applies in many of its semiotic details, the Holden Caulfield prototype has undergone some radical changes.

## Adolescence vs. Teenagerhood

The very idea of the *teenager*, and of the social connotations that this term has come to have, is, as mentioned, a relatively recent construct. Nature segments the life continuum into three biological periods: pre-reproductive, reproductive, and post-reproductive. The first crucial biological dividing line is, of course, *puberty* – the period during which an individual becomes physiologically capable of reproduction. Any other segmentation of this continuum has a social etiology. Categories such as *childhood, adolescence, adulthood,* and the like are concepts that reflect the ways in which cultures organize, and represent, what is essentially a continuous biological gestalt – the life span of a human being.

It is necessary to differentiate clearly between the terms *adolescence* and *teenagerhood.* The former refers to the psychosocial behaviours that are characteristic of all primates at puberty. As the etymology of the word implies (from Latin *adolescere,* 'to grow up'), it designates the behaviours set in motion by the onset of the reproductive capacity. A synonym for adolescent is *young adult. Teenagerhood,* on the other hand, refers to a socially constructed category superimposed on the life continuum by modern consumeristic culture. Throughout this book the terms *teenager* and *adolescent* will be used somewhat interchangeably, with the former generally focusing on the socio-semiotic characteristics of young people, and the latter on their psychosocial ones. As Helen Fisher (1992: 232) remarks, what I have designated as teenagerhood is 'a hallmark of the human animal, another divergence from our relatives, the apes.' Incidentally, the word *teenager* itself first appeared in the 1943–5 issue of the *Reader's Guide to Periodical Literature* (Rice 1990: 79).

The term *adolescens* ('adolescent') was used as far back as the Middle Ages to refer to any boy, irrespective of age, who began to work independently (Shahar 1992: 27). But in no sense did it have any of the psychosocial connotations that it has today. The basis for being categorized as an adolescens in medieval Europe was purely a matter of economic independence. Moreover, *adolescentia* ('adolescence') was considered to be an early period of maturity, not of transition, that lasted well into one's twenties and thirties.

As pointed out above, the idea of making adolescence a specific period for psychologists to study was proposed in

1904 by Stanley G. Hall. Hall put forward a theory of adolescence, known as *recapitulation theory*, which postulated that the development from childhood to adulthood inhered in a re-enactment of the sociobiological evolution of the human race. For Hall, the infant relived the animal stage, the adolescent the savage stage, and so on. Hall obviously assumed that the sociobiological history of humanity became a part of the genetic makeup of the individual human being. He also perceived adolescence as a period of *Sturm und Drang* ('storm and stress') in the sense of the term immortalized by Wolfgang Goethe in his 1774 novel, *The Sorrows of the Young Werther*.

Hall's sociobiological perspective is not as far-fetched as it might at first seem. Studying the ways in which children develop language, cognitive abilities, personality, and social comportment constitutes, arguably, an important means for gaining insight into the origin and evolution of human nature. During the 'Darwinian' nineteenth century this hypothesis was raised to the status of a biological law: *ontogeny recapitulates phylogeny*. As Milner (1990: 44) remarks, during that century it 'was considered one of the proofs of evolution.' For most of this century it was largely abandoned, having turned out to be untenable in some of its particulars, until Stephen Jay Gould's 1977 book, *Ontogeny and Phylogeny*, rekindled widespread interest in it. But even before the advent of Darwinism, the great Neapolitan philosopher Giambattista Vico (1688–1744) was already suggesting in his 1725 masterpiece, the *New Science* (see Bergin and Fisch 1984 for a translation), that the phylogenetic scenario is re-enacted in the mental, social, and verbal development of the child in a chronologically compressed way.

As Hall was formulating his ground-breaking ideas on adolescence, one concomitantly finds interspersed throughout the writings of the founder of psychoanalysis, Sigmund Freud (1856–1939), case-studies of young adults who claimed to have been highly influenced by their early childhood experiences. The psychologist who has been most influenced by Freud's analyses of adolescents, and who has become one of the leading researchers on the psychosocial features of adolescence since mid century, is Erik Erikson (e.g., 1950, 1968). Erikson has noted that the pubescent human being passes universally through developmental phases which eventually lead to a sense of self-worth or, as he calls it, 'ego identity.' Although it is largely a natural biological tendency, Erikson has suggested that this developmental process is given its particular shape by the culture in which the individual is reared. Accordingly, the adolescent is purported to search for an identity through 'role diffusion,' (i.e., through some form of identification with a 'hero' or a 'leader') to the extent of, paradoxically, even losing his or her own developing identity.

One who has become known even beyond the confines of academe for his study of human mental growth and development is the Swiss psychologist Jean Piaget (1896–1980). Piaget's work on the evolution of the cognitive functions in terms of how they are formed (e.g., Piaget 1969; Piaget and Inhelder 1969) exemplifies how the mind–body vinculum governs the ontogenesis of personality. The three stages of development that Piaget posited – sensory-motor, concrete operations, and formal-logical thinking – have become widely accepted as the primary biological milestones en route to cognitive and personality development. Piaget has shown, in a phrase, that humans progress from a sensory and concrete stage of mind to a reflective and abstract one. Around the age of two, according to Piaget's observations, children start to develop symbolic abilities derived from mental images. As these become more dynamic, they prepare the child for more abstract thinking. Knowledge in the child emerges in terms of a direct relation to events in the immediate environment. Self-knowledge arises later. For the present purposes, it is important to note that, according to Piaget, the final stage of development begins at early adolescence when the human being becomes capable of abstract symbolism, making him or her highly susceptible to the universe of social *semiosis*, to the world of socially sensitive symbol- and image-making.

Critics of Piaget's theory perceived in it a certain determinism and an overemphasis on cognitive processes at the expense of affect or emotion. And it is in having combined the affective and social dimensions with cognitive growth that, in my view, the work of both Vygotsky (e.g., 1961, 1984) and Bruner (e.g., 1986, 1990) can be deployed to supplement and balance out Piagetian psychology. The Russian psychologist L.S. Vygotsky (1896–1934) proposed developmental stages that went from external (physical and social) actions towards internal cognitive constructions and interior speech, via the mind's ability to construct images of external reality. His definition of speech as a 'microcosm of consciousness' was particularly reflective of his viewpoint. He saw language as a kind of 'symbolic modelling device,' which became the dominant mode of cognition after children became adolescents.

The great cognitive psychologist Jerome Bruner has suggested that the construction of the intellect starts with an 'enactive' stage, passes through an 'iconic' stage, and finally reaches a 'symbolic' stage. Corporeal action, imagination, and abstract thought are the chronologically related stages through which each child passes on the way to mature thinking: for example, the child first employs nonverbal symbols (action, play, drawing, painting, music, etc.), then imaginative constructs (narratives, fables, dramatizations, etc.), and finally oral expression and creative writing on the road to the formation of abstract thought.

It is relevant here to go back once again to Vico, the philosopher who seems to have anticipated much of the current work in the human sciences. As Robert Di Pietro (1973: 411) remarked two decades ago, for Vico it was through the study of language that cultural and human development could be deciphered: '[Vico] felt that societal changes as evidenced in man's language were similar to the stages through which man passes in his own maturation. Thus, we can characterize language as capable of reflecting the child's fear of the unknown, the adolescent's admiration for heroes, and the adult's use of reasoning powers.'

While contemporary psychologists and linguists may quibble over the exactitude of the individual phylogenetic ages posited by Vico, over his whimsical word etymologies, or over the apparent 'roundaboutness' with which he exposes his ideas (e.g., Hall 1963), there would seem to be little disagreement today over his cyclical theory of human ontogenetic development as reflective of phylogenetic evolutionary stages. According to Vico, human societies progress from barbarism to civilization and then back to barbarism. The term 'barbarism' in Vico refers simply to a primitive stage of civilization. In the first stage – which he called the 'age of the gods' – religion, burial rites, the family, and other basic institutions emerge to lay the foundations of human culture. He called this primordial phase of humanity the age of the 'gods' because he saw the first reflective humans as being filled with an intense fear of natural phenomena such as thunder and lightning. Not possessing the knowledge to understand or 'explain' such environmental events, the first humans ascribed them to awesome and frightful 'gods' or 'divine' creatures – hence the designation 'age of the gods.' Vico called the first speakers 'poets,' which etymologically means 'makers.' They used language to create likenesses among the things in the world and, therefore, to create new, context-free, associations. In the succeeding 'age of heroes,' a dominant class of humans – the 'heroes' of the evolving culture – emerges, typically, to subjugate the common people. These are men with great physical prowess who inspire fear and admiration in the common people. The latter typically ascribe divine powers to these 'nobles.' After a period of domination, a third stage – the 'age of men or equals' –

invariably takes shape in which the common people rise up and win equality; but in the process society begins to disintegrate as it returns to a more vile and violent form of barbarism (rational or reflective barbarism). This, according to Vico, is the natural 'course' of human civilized cultures – a course that is not linear and endlessly progressive, but cyclical and finite. Cultures are born and cultures die. They do not go on forever; they are 'killed' by their barbarism of reflection, so to speak. But in their 'death' they are going to be 'reborn' with a more ethical form of humanity.

When viewed cumulatively, the developmental literature suggests that it would not be too far-fetched to compare the child's first words to those of Vico's 'poets.' During their first stages of emerging consciousness, children develop a vocabulary that reflects a need to understand beings, objects, and events in terms of their perceptual attributes. Children then pass typically through a secondary stage during which they become totally wrapped up in the heroic figures that their specific cultures make available to them. It is during this 'heroic' stage that adolescence emerges as the primary mental and affective gestalt in humans.

Since Stanley G. Hall's pioneering work, psychologists have gone on to catalogue the features that characterize the physical, emotional, and social attainment of adolescence. It is now largely thought that the psychosocial changes noticed at puberty are intermeshed with changes in bodily appearance and function. This is why the adolescent becomes obsessively concerned about his or her physical appearance. Inhabiting a strange new body, the adolescent starts to feel awkward, anxious, guilty (or afraid) of certain physical desires and feelings, and totally enwrapped in his or her developing social consciousness – an intense and all-pervasive awareness of, and sensitivity to, what others think of him or her. Membership in a peer group becomes the primary locus within which the adolescent seeks temporary shelter from the ravaging effects of his or her heightened consciousness of self. The peer group serves, at first, as a kind of asylum from the new burdens emanating from social cognition. It allows the adolescent an opportunity to 'blend in' with peers who are in the same frame of mind and literally to efface his or her self from his or her bodily manifestations (for detailed and fairly recent surveys of the work on the social psychology of adolescence, see, for instance, Desjarlais and Rackauskas 1986; Coleman and Hendry 1990; and Rice 1990).

It is worth emphasizing at this point that the psychological research on adolescence has made it abundantly clear, when looked at synthetically and comparatively, that the behaviours coinciding with the advent of puberty are determined by an interaction between biological tendencies and cultural factors. As Hutchison (1990: 79–82) has perceptively pointed out, ever since the advent of scientific psychology in the previous century there have emerged two radically different views of human development – environmentalism vs. innatism. In fact these are really no more than modern versions of the empiricist and rationalist perspectives which have been debated passionately throughout the history of Western philosophy. According to one point of view, humans are born with their minds a tabula rasa. They then assume their nature 'in response to the stimuli they encounter in their environment' (Hutchison 1990: 79). Humans are thus depicted as malleable organisms – as 'sponges' – constantly being shaped by environmental input. The behaviourist movement in psychology in this century has epitomized this viewpoint. The other perspective contends that humans are indeed malleable, but that they are not born with an 'empty slate.' Rather, in the terminology of contemporary neuroscience, they are perceived to be 'hard-wired' from birth to behave in certain ways.

Such outlooks also entail partisan views of how we develop mentally and socially. According to behaviourists, development is a result of the build-up of response patterns to environmental inputs. While most people seem intuitively more inclined to believe this view – that we are shaped by what we are exposed to – those within the cognitive and social sciences who study how people think, behave, and learn have largely abandoned the behaviourist viewpoint and have, as a consequence, become oriented towards discovering the 'cognitive mechanisms' that are supposedly tied to an innate 'hard-wiring' in the brain. In this scenario, the human being is conceived to be a 'processor' of input. Humans are purported to have no more control over how they understand and handle input than they do over their breathing. Of course, they can set up obstacles to block the functioning of their input-processing mechanisms, just as they can prevent themselves from breathing. They can refuse to process input by shutting themselves off from what is happening around them. But they cannot change their hard-wired propensities in any radical way.

In my opinion, both views – that of humans as sponges and that of humans as input-processors – are partially correct. The truth probably lies in the fact that we are both biologically inclined towards certain behaviours and invariably influenced by the ways in which the environment impacts upon us.

So, while it might be true that adolescence is a biologically segmentable stage in the life continuum of human beings (and of all primates for that matter), it is not true that teenagerhood is its inevitable offshoot. Anthropologists have, in fact, found that in many cultures the kinds of behaviours that we associate with North American teenagers simply do not exist. By mid century Margaret Mead (1950) had assembled a large body of data on Samoan society which showed that the adolescent experiences of North American culture were not unavoidable. Mead discovered that Samoan children followed a continuous growth pattern, with no abrupt changes from one age to the other. Simply put, the traditional Samoan culture might be said to have adolescents in the sense defined by psychologists – juveniles capable of reproduction – but it does not have the kinds of individuals whom we immediately recognize as teenagers. Moreover, Mead found that the period that psychologists call adolescence need not be stormy or stressful. Unlike Freud and Hall, she maintained that culture has much more effect on the emergence of adolescent psychosocial behaviours than can be accounted for primarily by biology.

The crystallization of the teenage persona and of its supporting subculture can be traced to the fifties. In most of the Western world, the appearance of this new 'social animal' has led to significant changes in social structure and economic behaviour. It has also had a notable influence on the processes that characterize the child's psychosocial development at puberty. As a social construct, teenagerhood has engendered its own pattern of semiosis: it has generated its own distinct and easily recognizable *symbology*, or modalities of symbolic thinking and acting that children approaching puberty acquire unconsciously from their social environment. Teenage behaviour is, above all else, socially coded behaviour deriving its characteristic features from a process that can be called *signifying osmosis*. This is a signifying, or meaning-making, mode of acting or conducting oneself that is acquired in relation to socially powerful stimuli. Thus, for example, the typical bodily postures, facial expressions, emotional outbursts, modes of dress, and discourse features that have come to characterize teenage demeanour in general can be said to be anchored in behavioural patterns that are both *significant* – socially meaningful – and *signifying* – meaning-making – to the peer group. These behavioural patterns take shape in the individual as he or she gains a new and powerful form of social cognition at puberty. Teenagers literally 'pick up' their ways of acting and thinking from each other so as to demonstrate adherence and conformity to peer-generated and peer-sanctioned models of behaviour.

## J.D. Salinger's *Catcher in the Rye*

The first to understand deeply, and to capture superbly in fiction, the emerging phenomenon of teenagerhood in the late forties and early fifties was the contemporary novelist, J.D. Salinger (1919– ). In his masterpiece, *The Catcher in the Rye*, the character of Holden Caulfield is the prototype of the contemporary rebellious and confused teenager. Although the book came out in 1951, various portions of it were published as far back as 1945 in *Collier's* and *The New Yorker*. Teenagerhood also imbues the thematic texture of Salinger's other works – *Nine Stories* (1953), *Franny and Zooey* (1961), *Raise High the Roof Beam, Carpenters* (1963), and *Seymour: An Introduction* (1963).

*The Catcher in the Rye* is a marvellous portrait of the teenage persona, or more accurately, of the various *personae* that were beginning to populate the emerging teenage subculture of the late forties and early fifties. Sixteen-year-old Holden Caulfield, a troubled, troublesome, and insubordinate adolescent who has recently been suspended from his preparatory school and placed in a sanitarium, retells to a psychiatrist the events of the few days leading up to his Christmas vacation. Holden is disgusted by the hypocrisy of society and his narrative account unveils the emotional essence of the idealistic adolescent mind – a mind disgusted by phoniness, insensitivity, self-indulgence, and stupidity. Holden Caulfield is the prototype of the egocentric adolescent psyche – self-centred and repulsed by the social masks that people wear and by the routine and dreary speech habits they constantly exhibit.

In a sense, the persona of Holden Caulfield is a contemporary continuation of a figure which has a long social and literary tradition in our culture. Caulfield's narrative ancestry can be traced to the adolescent characters found in Goethe's *Werther* (1774), Dostoyevsky's *Raw Youth* (1875), more recently translated as *The Adolescent*, Tarkington's *Seventeen* (1916), and similar literary creations. But in a fundamental way, Holden Caulfield is quite different. Holden speaks a language uniquely his own, suffused with the voice-rhythms, turns-of-phrase, and expressions of modern adolescence. He uses this language strategically to re-create the world around him. The reader is thus 'shown' the world through the particular perspective of a sixteen-year-old teenager.

The novel also paints portraits of other teenage personae. There is Robert Ackley, Holden's dorm mate at school, whose disgusting habits are not atypical of what contemporary teens call *dork* or *geek* behaviours. Ackley is teenagerhood's first geek, a physically repulsive character who is incapable of masking his awkward and unhygienic appearance:

He was one of the very, very tall, round-shouldered guys – he was about six four – with lousy teeth. The whole time he roomed next to me, I never even once saw him brush his teeth. They always looked mossy and awful, and he damn near made you sick if you saw him in the dining room with his mouth full of mashed potatoes and peas or something. Besides that, he had a lot of pimples. Not just on his forehead or his chin, like most guys, but all over his whole face. And not only that, he had a terrible personality. (Salinger 1951: 19)

It is interesting to note that Salinger's humorous image of 'pimples' as detractors of facial appearance constitutes one of the first ever interpretive keys to understanding the nature of the teenager's self-consciousness and inordinate preoccupation with appearance. Pimples, like any other kind of facial blemish, are symbolic markers for teens. Ackley is the incarnation of ugliness, as seen through the metonym of a pimply complexion.

Then there is Ward Stradlater, Holden's roommate, who

constitutes the first literary depiction of *coolness:* 'He always *looked* good when he was finished fixing himself up, but he was a secret slob anyway, if you knew him the way I did. The reason he fixed himself up to look good was because he was madly in love with himself. He thought he was the handsomest guy in the Western hemisphere.' (Salinger 1951: 27)

Holden Caulfield, Ackley, Stradlater, and the other young people in the novel speak, act, and think like teenagers in the modern sense of the word. For the first time ever in Western fiction, the *teenager* had been given a narrative identity. Holden Caulfield was a new persona. As Doherty (1988: 46) remarks, it was soon after the publication of Salinger's ground-breaking novel that 'in the marketplace and the media, at home and at school, the teenager came to be counted a special animal requiring special handling.'

**The Fifties**

My history of teenagerhood is divided arbitrarily into decades. Needless to say, the evolution of contemporary teenagerhood is the result of an unbroken historical continuity. The practice of referring to decades is consistent, however, with popular perceptions. When one thinks of 'the fifties,' images of sock hops, 'American Bandstand,' Elvis Presley, and the ritual of the sixteenth-birthday party come immediately to mind; and when one contemplates 'the sixties,' one cannot help but recall images of the hippie movement, the Beatles, and the general rebellious mood of adolescents.

It was the fifties that saw the unprecedented publication of guidebooks such as Baruch's *How to Live with Your Teenager* (1953) and Landis's *Understanding Teenagers* (1955). These bore witness to the fact that teenagerhood was starting to be perceived in North America as a special problem. The same decade also saw the appearance of the first magazines dedicated solely to teenagers (*Dig, Teen, Teen World, Sixteen, Teen Romances*, etc.). These were also unprecedented, since, as Doherty (1988: 59) comments, they constituted, for the first time ever, publications that 'addressed the teenager as a peer and advised him – or more often her – on how to become a more attractive and popular teenager.'

Before the fifties, there were no songs, books, magazines, or movies dealing with, or aimed at, teenage audiences. With the rise of television and of the record industry in the fifties, white, middle-class teenagers were soon courted by the media, because of the amount of leisure time they had and their propensity to consume and spend. By the mid fifties the courtship of the teenage consumer by the media and various entertainment industries (especially the record and movie ones) began in full earnest. Songs and movies became progressively juvenilized in content. The various 'Hit Parades' on radio started to reflect a new focus on the teenage subculture as the primary audience. Television dance programs, like 'American Bandstand,' which was first broadcast in August 1957, made instant celebrities of the teenage dancers who performed on them. As Stern and Stern (1992: 15) observe, 'American Bandstand' in particular was the first true program exclusively for teens on television: 'It was for teens only; and it heralded the arrival of a new generation eager to embrace a pop culture of its own.'

'Hanging out' after school to socialize with peers became a daily event. And the Saturday-night party with school friends crystallized as an event of great significance to the social life of the teenager. The rituals performed at such social gatherings included the smoking of cigarettes, the consumption of alcohol, and a casual engagement in sexual activities. Missing a Saturday-night party was perceived to be a blight on a teenager's reputation.

The first teenagers also came to have their own music, *rock and roll*, a term which clearly connotes the verve and bodily rhythms connected with pubescence. The birth of rock is usually traced to the 1955 hit song by Bill Haley and the Comets, 'Rock Around the Clock.' By 1956, with the emergence of Elvis Presley as the first rock deity, it became clear that rock and roll was much more than just a new form of musical entertainment. As Greenwald (1992: 7) aptly puts it, rock and roll was, and continues to be, 'clothing and hair styles, social criticism, a manifestation of sociological forces, and an agent of change.' The first true 'mythical heroes' of the teenage subculture were rock and roll artists. Male singers like Elvis Presley, Little Richard, Jerry Lee Lewis, Chuck Berry, Sam Cooke, James Brown, Buddy Holly, the Everly Brothers, and many more, brought adolescent girls to tearful frenzy as they swung their hips in rhythmic osmosis of sexual movements. Female rock stars like Annette Funicello and Connie Francis made pubescent boys and girls swoon. This was the era of the 'crush,' of falling in love with love itself through the medium of a new, powerful mode of sexual-aesthetic experience – rock and roll.

Perhaps no one embodied the new mythology more than Elvis Presley. At every live performance teenage girls screamed, fainted, languished, and attempted to reach and touch Elvis on stage. After appearing on the 'Ed Sullivan Show' in 1956, he became an instant teen idol – a 'Vichian hero' – in the eyes of teenagers throughout North America, and, at the same time, a menacing, evil force in the eyes of countless parents. Elvis Presley also became the first model of male *coolness*. His bodily movements, facial expressions (especially his peculiar raised lip twitch), hairstyle, verbal drawl, became the discrete features of coolness for male teens. The 'Stradlaters' of the mid fifties were Elvis Presley clones. Some of them, who are still alive today, continue to cling to the Elvis Presley model of physical appearance. Since Elvis's death in 1977, the 'king of rock and roll' lives on as a myth, worshipped and venerated through television serials, Elvis impersonators, reissues of his records, and memorabilia. Such is the emotive force of teenagerhood. Long after one's teen years have ended, the symbology and behavioural models acquired during this period persist and endure.

Following in Elvis's footsteps was Jerry Lee Lewis, who transformed the sensual innuendoes of Elvis's 'All Shook Up' (1956) into blatant carnal sexuality in such hits as 'Whole Lotta Shakin' Goin' On' (1957), 'Great Balls of Fire' (1958), and 'Breathless' (1958). Lewis's lyrics and incessant rhythms came forward to evoke bodily feelings in ways that were reminiscent of pagan sexual rites. Presley and Lewis thrilled teens and petrified parents. They were created and sustained as heroes of the new subculture by the media. North American culture was fast becoming a 'mediated' one.

Television turned 'softer' rock stars like Ricky Nelson, one of the Nelson teens on the popular sitcom 'The Adventures of Ozzie and Harriet,' into overnight successes. Incidentally, this sitcom was one of the first to deal specifically with the problems of raising teenage children (two sons in this case) in the context of the new teenage subculture. Through media images, rock stars influenced hairstyles (e.g., the Elvis sideburns), introduced clothing fashions (e.g., the 'white buck' shoes popularized by Pat Boone), and started dance crazes (such as 'hop dancing,' introduced by Danny and the Juniors with their 1958 hit 'At the Hop'). They became the primary shapers of the new symbology associated with teenagerhood.

An incident that occurred in the winter of 1958 is indicative of the sway and emotive effect that the new mythical heroes of rock and roll held over the 'first generation' of teenagers. Three highly successful singers, Buddy Holly, Ritchie Valens, and the 'Big Bopper' were killed in an airplane crash on the way to a rock concert. Their tragic death was treated by the media as an event of mythic proportions. Their songs, which would have faded away into the 'oldies' category in a short period of time, became classics of great emotional power and import. Teenage girls and boys cried incessantly as they heard their fallen heroes live on mythologically through the magic of audio reproduction. Photographs and posters of the three heroes were transformed into icons of veneration and hung on bedroom walls throughout North America.

By the late fifties, the radio, television, cinema, and record industries had firmly entrenched teenagerhood as a *sui generis* way of life. Children reaching puberty by, say, 1959 seemed to become transformed overnight into gum-chewing, party-going, rock and roll enthusiasts, who lived through the immediacy of the present moment. Affluent teenage girls in particular – called 'bobby-soxers' – became a primary target of media moguls. Well-groomed male teen idols such as Frankie Avalon, Fabian, Paul Anka, Bobby Rydell, and Ricky Nelson, with their new 'syrupy' sound (in contrast to the hard-driving sexual rhythms of Elvis Presley or Little Richard), were created by the media and entertainment industries specifically for the bobby-soxer. Their songs spoke of 'puppy love,' of 'sweet kisses,' not of 'breathlessness' or of 'shaking' à la Jerry Lee Lewis. Seen as much 'safer' by parents of female teens, and by the self-appointed moral guardians of society, the music of these teenage crooners became the mainstream music of the era.

So by the end of the fifties the teenage persona was developing a 'split personality.' Elvis was still around, but he was losing his supremacy. The new breed of male teen idols displayed a toned-down and more socially acceptable form of coolness. The allegiance of teens waffled from one brand of symbology (the Elvis kind) to the other (the Fabian kind). Perhaps it was the movie idol James Dean who best manifested both sides of this new personality. Physically, he resembled one of the new teen idols, well-groomed and mild-mannered. But below this veneer, he exuded the rebelliousness and sexuality of Elvis. James Dean was Elvis Presley and Fabian wrapped into one. Teenagerhood was clearly on the verge of a radical change.

## The Sixties

The early sixties institutionalized even further much of the symbology associated with fifties-style teenagerhood. Modifying one's physical appearance (hairstyle, dress codes, etc.) to conform to peer-sanctioned models continued to characterize the passage from childhood to teenagerhood at puberty. Saturday-night parties were regularized, and the pressure to attend them increased. Rock music, smoking, and hanging out were entrenched even deeper as primary constituents of teen symbology.

But many significant changes to the constantly evolving symbology were also set in motion. Whereas in the fifties the sixteenth-birthday party marked the symbolic transition from teenagerhood to late adolescence and, thus, to more mature forms of behaviour, by the mid sixties this ritualistic breakpoint was extended by a few years to encompass the entire high school period. The high school environment was becoming more and more a locus for socialization, providing the milieu within which teenagers centred more and more of their lives. It came to constitute a community in the ethnographic sense of the word: in other words, it was increasingly evolving into a self-contained social system within the larger societal framework. What Lynd and Lynd (1929: 24) had observed decades earlier became particularly applicable to teenage life in the sixties: 'The high school, with its athletics, clubs, sororities and fraternities, dances and parties, and other extracurricular activities is a fairly complete social cosmos in itself, and about this city within a city the social life of the intermediate generation centers.' The daily life of a sixties teenager was becoming anchored within this 'social cosmos,' as the Lynds characterized it. Teenagers started to see the high school context as the central locus for gaining and maintaining social status, primarily through symbolic codes, actions, and behaviours that were deemed to be socially advantageous by the peer group. Teenagers sought, like never before, to gain overall acceptance, status, and prestige within the high school through a skilful manipulation of the symbology of coolness.

Perhaps the greatest change that took shape in the sixties was a new propensity to become part of a clique within in the school. The teenage world described by Holden Caulfield was a monolithic one – the Ackleys and the Stradlaters were its prototypes. Now, although there continued to be a general teenage subculture in society at large, the cliquing phenomenon brought about a new diversification and sophistication in teenage symbology and behaviour. Nowhere was this reflected more than in the growing differentiation and sophistication in musical preferences. In the fifties Elvis Presley was the 'king' of rock, who 'reigned' over all his teen 'subjects.' By the mid sixties the king was dethroned, and macho teen idols were demolished. The *rock group* emerged as a new imparter of diversified value systems, symbologies, and behavioural codes. The focus had shifted from the individual to the group. In the fifties, there was *one* hit parade for everyone. Now, there were several hit parades, reflecting highly differentiated musical styles – *Motown, Memphis soul, Surf rock*, and so on. Teenagers associated themselves more and more with specific musical styles and groups, not only with individual performers, of which there continued nevertheless to be many (e.g., Wilson Pickett, Aretha Franklin, Stevie Wonder, Marvin Gaye, Jackie Wilson, to mention some of the better known and remembered ones). Rock was also becoming less and less the privileged domain of male stars. 'Girl groups,' such as the Chantels, the Crystals, the Shirelles, the Supremes, and the Marvellettes were coming more and more to the forefront.

From the mid sixties onwards, rock and roll was also becoming *the* primary artistic medium for expressing revolutionary social and political ideas. It was no longer just music to dance to or to fall in love by. The radical 'hippie' movement of the sixties was propelled by rock and roll. Its artistic voices included performers and bands such as Bob Dylan, Joan Baez, Joe Cocker, Van Morrison, Simon & Garfunkel, the Mamas and the Papas, the Band, the Rolling Stones, Credence Clearwater Revival, the Doors, Jimi Hendrix, the Byrds, Procul Harum, Pink Floyd, and the Beatles. These new voices denounced apathy, warmongering, racism, stereotyping, and other social ills. By the end of the sixties, and the birth of *hard rock* in the hard-driving, grim, violent rhythms of Steppenwolf and Led Zeppelin, it became obvious that the transformation that the teenage persona had undergone in a little more than a decade was a radical one indeed. The advent of hard rock onto the scene was a harbinger of the route teenagerhood was to embark on from the seventies to the present day.

The influence of the British rock group the Beatles on this whole transformational process cannot be ignored. Elvis Presley was the figurehead of the teenage subculture in the fifties; similarly, the Beatles came to epitomize the transformation this subculture had undergone in the sixties. Coming out of the working slums of Liverpool in the early sixties, by the time they produced the album *Sergeant Pepper's Lonely Hearts Club Band* in 1967, the four Beatles – Paul McCartney, John Lennon, George Harrison, and Ringo Starr – had raised rock and roll to the level of high musical art. Their long hair and their mode of dress became the general models of coolness in the mid sixties. 'Beatlemania' was as intense as 'Elvismania' had been a decade earlier. The Beatles were the inheritors of Elvis's throne. But by the time of the albums *Rubber Soul* (1965) and *Sergeant Pepper* (1967), the Beatles had revolutionized teenagerhood, temporarily imbuing it with a much more mature and profound character. Indeed, it might be said that *Rubber Soul* and *Sergeant Pepper* gave impetus to, if not generated, the entire hippie and counter-culture movement (see also Whiteley 1992 on the association between sixties rock and the counter-culture). The musical revolution they started made the rock concert, especially the 'open-air' concert, a momentous ideological event. Drugs were consumed openly at such concerts to induce or heighten the aesthetic experience of the whole event. 'Free love' was practised openly. By the end of the decade, rock operas, such as *Tommy* (1969) by the Who, were being considered as serious works of musical art by mainstream classical music critics.

Running parallel to these new trends, Elvis Presley was making movies that were transforming him into a cinema star for the 'ex-teenagers' of the fifties. By the way these ex-teenagers clung to their fifties memories it was becoming increasingly obvious that teenagerhood had developed into a force that was permanently changing the sociology of modern culture. More and more people maintained and cherished their teenage symbology well beyond adolescence. Rock music was becoming more and more mainstream music. Teenage symbologies were becoming mainstream symbologies. And while all this was going on, the new generation of teenagers sought out new symbols and codes to keep their identities different from those of the ex-teenagers.

**The Seventies and Eighties**

During the seventies and eighties, hanging out, partying – with alcohol and drugs becoming intrinsic features of the party scene – and 'cliquing' continued to characterize the teen subculture at large. Becoming *cool* was now being perceived to be a prerequisite for children entering junior high and high school. But the specific characteristics of coolness varied widely from school to school, from clique to clique. The media was becoming saturated with teenagers. Today, it has become virtually impossible to find a new song, movie, or television program which does not deal with, or is not aimed at, teenagers or ex-teenagers. The number of magazines, books, and scientific journals dealing with problems of teenagerhood is overwhelming. It should also be pointed out that while the first generation of teenagers in the fifties belonged primarily to an affluent, white middle class – Holden Caulfield did, after all, go to a preparatory school – by the seventies teenagerhood had become a classless phenomenon.

The seventies and eighties saw the entrenchment of hard and dissonant musical styles, each entailing specific dress and behavioural codes, embodied by *hard rock* performers and bands like Frank Zappa and Alice Cooper, by *heavy metal* bands like Black Sabbath, Metallica, Motley Crüe, the Cult, Bon Jovi, Van Halen, Iron Maiden, and Guns N' Roses, by *punk* bands like the Sex Pistols, the Ramones, and the Viletones, and by *new wave* performers and bands like Blondie, The Police, and Elvis Costello. The very names of a number of these bands instilled, and continue to instil, fear into some parents and self-appointed protectors of the common good. The records, tapes, and compact discs of some of these bands have often come under the scrutiny of censorship-minded groups because of the explicit sexual and satanic themes they apparently glorify. The fashions that such performers have introduced also evoke disapprobation and condemnation from some people. These include black leather and black clothes generally, pentagram pendants, earrings for males, and very long hair.

Of particular concern to society at large in the mid seventies was the emergence of the punk movement. Those who called themselves 'punks' were British teens who came, at first, from the working class. Feeling alienated from mainstream culture, they came forward to threaten the social order by inveighing violently against it through their messages and actions. They pitted themselves in direct opposition to society; they were anti-bourgeois and anti-capitalist. Their performances were deliberately violent and confrontational. Members of punk rock bands spat on their audiences, mutilated themselves with knives, damaged the props on stage and in the hall, and incited their audiences to do the same. The fashion trends they introduced emphasized degradation. They introduced the craze for chains, dog collars, black clothes, army boots, and hairstyles which ranged from shaved heads to the wild-looking 'Mohawk' hairdos in every colour imaginable. Their music was the rock equivalent of Andy Warhol's sculptures or of John Cage's compositions: it was aleatory and 'do-it-yourself.' Musicians played notes, banged their guitars, shouted, burped, urinated, and bellowed at will on stage to a basic rhythmic pulsating beat.

These were, and continue to be, worrisome offshoots of teenagerhood. But it is my view that the trend in the seventies and eighties towards these musical styles and symbologies proclaiming violence, satanism, and destruction was, and continues to be, a veneer for a new strain of sexuality and rebellion bent on breaking down the traditional dichotomies of mainstream culture. This was nowhere so obvious as in what became a cult film in the mid seventies, *The Rocky Horror Picture Show*. At one level the movie was a parody of the fifties rock movement. As Greenwald (1992: 53) remarks, it was an attempt 'to shock by departing from the tradition of rock and roll machismo established by Elvis'; but at a deeper level it vaunted a new sexuality that favored 'makeup, cross dressing, and an overall smearing of the lines between the sexes.' This blurring of gender and social roles was also embodied in the hard rock band Kiss throughout the seventies. Their performances on stage were designed to shock adults and attract the new type of teen. Each member of the band adopted a comic-book persona – a glamour boy, an alien from outer space, a tomcat, and a sex-crazed Kabuki monster. They wore makeup and their stage act included fire-eating, smoke bombs, hydraulic lifts, and the smashing of instruments.

Running parallel to this 'hard movement,' associated in

large part with lower-class teenagers within the general teenage subculture, was the invention and emergence of 'disco' music, epitomized in the 1978 movie *Saturday Night Fever* starring John Travolta. The title of this movie captured the essence of what the Saturday-night party mood had become among seventies teenagers – a feverish need to be with one's peers engaged in sexual ritualizing through dance. This dimension of the teenage personality, which was attenuated temporarily in the early eighties, has been revived in the *house* music of the late eighties. Obviously, the need to be a participant at some kind of Saturday-night 'event' – a disco, a party, or some other type of get-together with peers – has become a powerful shaper of behaviour in the contemporary teenager. The disco scene, as an unabashed celebration of sexuality, was evocative of a pagan hedonistic rite purified culturally by the glitter and glitz of high fashion. Bands and performers like Chic, the Village People, Donna Summer, and KC & the Sunshine Band catered to a specific subgroup of primarily affluent, middle-class teenagers. Others rejected disco with the expression 'disco sucks!' It was seen by many other teens as superficial and much too acceptable to the adult culture.

The fact that during the seventies and eighties the teenage subculture was continuing to split up into many factions was evidenced by hard rock, punk rock, disco, and other musical styles coexisting side by side in the media. Symbologically, each faction demanded its own dress and behavioural codes. There were *pop* musicians (e.g., Elton John, Madonna, Wham, Duran Duran, and Michael Jackson), *jazz* and *blues* musicians (e.g., Santana, Chicago, Anita Baker, Steely Dan), *southern rock* musicians (e.g., the Allman Brothers and Lynyrd Skynyrd), *rock* musicians (e.g., Eric Clapton, Bruce Springsteen), *folk* musicians (e.g., Carole King, Joni Mitchell, Linda Ronstadt, James Taylor), and *soul* and *funk* musicians (e.g., Rufus, the Ohio Players, Kool & the Gang, Sly & the Family Stone, Earth, Wind and

Fire). The history of teenagerhood, in all its diversity and complexity, is reflected in the history of rock and roll.

To illustrate how radically teenagerhood had changed in the seventies and eighties, consider two performers who became mythic heroes in that era – Michael Jackson and Madonna. There was no doubt about the masculinity and machismo of Elvis Presley. This feature of his personality was the key ingredient used by the media to construct his mythology and a recognizable iconology. But the world had undergone a drastic mutation by the seventies and eighties. Both Michael Jackson and Madonna became heroes in large part because of the radically different sexual personae they represented. With his many eccentricities, Jackson became a symbol of hermaphroditism. Extolling both male and female sexual characteristics at once, as well as black and white racial qualities (achieved through extensive cosmetic surgery to his face), Michael Jackson has come to personify our culture's obsession with sexuality – with its nature, role, and evolution. Unlike Prince, who symbolizes a more contemporary version of machismo, Jackson straddles the heterosexual fence, tantalizing his audiences to join him on either the homosexual or bisexual sides. Whether it is themes like masturbation in his 1983 hit *Beat It* (a metaphor for male masturbation), or androgyny in his late eighties album *Bad*, Michael Jackson symbolizes our fascination with prurience and obscenity.

Madonna came on to the teenage scene in 1983. Her songs introduced a reactionary tinge to the feminist movement in North American society. Songs such as *Like a Virgin*, *Material Girl*, and *Dress You Up*, which blatantly portrayed females as objectified sexual beings, topped the hit-parade charts, to the chagrin and dismay of leading feminists. Madonna combined a Marilyn Monroe 'sex-kitten' pose with a compelling and urgent sensuality. But it was an aloof and distant form of sexuality that Madonna displayed. It had (and continues to have) a peep-show quality suited for a voyeuristic society that seems to prefer a mediated form of sexuality to the real thing.

## The Post-modern Teenager

As I write, current musical preferences (e.g., *house, rap, hard rock*, etc.) have become even more coded and aimed at specific kinds of teen cliques; the high school has become even more of a locus for socialization, for choosing one's peers, for partying, for abandoning oneself, in a phrase, to the 'immediacy of the symbolic moment.' There is one new trend in music, however, that is particularly interesting from a sociological standpoint: namely, an emphasis on, and fascination with, African-American musical styles.

There is now a widespread *reggae* movement, which, although it gained momentum during the late eighties, is really one that can be traced back several decades. The introduction of African-based musical styles into the North American teen subculture goes as far back as 1961 when the Tokens recorded the highly popular song 'The Lion Sleeps Tonight.' The Beatles imitated the reggae style in their 1968 song 'Ob-La-Di, Ob-La-Da.' During the seventies and eighties, Jamaican reggae rhythms and melodies found their way into the songs of Sting and The Police. In 1986 Paul Simon made African musical texture an intrinsic part of his *Graceland* album.

But it is the rap movement that has come predominantly to the forefront, especially among African-American teenagers who have made it their primary artistic medium for self-expression. The lyrics of such composers as Public Enemy and Ice Cube assail the modern ideological and sociological status quo, threatening to transform it radically. At the same time that the disco mentality is being re-evoked in the house music of the dance-club scene, rap music has become a kind of standard-bearer and barometer of general trends within the teenage subculture at large. The term *rap* derives from the fact that in the dance halls of Harlem and the South Bronx in the mid seventies disc jockeys played an eclectic mix of funk, soul, hard rock, and other musical styles to entertain their audiences. The more enthusiastic members of audiences would sing-song rhymes, exhorting other teens to dance and 'get into it.' These 'rapping' exhortations started to crop up all over New York, taking on reggae variations, and soon becoming a major focus of African-American rock artists.

In becoming part of the mainstream, rap music has vindicated the often-ignored role played by African-American music in the birth of rock. As Wicke (1987: 16) has put it: 'In musical terms rock's emergence as a form of mass communication was signalled by the radical re-orientation of the development of pop music towards the traditions of Afro-American music in the USA.' The music of Elvis Presley, Chuck Berry, and others was the result of this re-orientation.

The rap scene has also introduced many new fashion trends into the contemporary teen subculture, including African dashikis, shell necklaces, Kangol caps, sweat suits, unlaced hi-top sneakers, gold chains, and capped teeth. As Greenwald (1992: 188) observes, rap quickly became allied, visually and ideologically, with African-American culture, 'including the colorful graffiti murals that adorned subway cars and the acrobatics of break dancers spinning on a piece of cardboard for small change.'

But despite the prominence that the rap movement has achieved, there is now, as never before, a true smorgasbord of musical styles from which to choose as one enters teenagerhood. Moreover, as I see it, the symbology of this social phenomenon is becoming more and more *post-modern*.

What is *post-modernism*? Like the tramps in Samuel Beckett's 1949 play, *Waiting for Godot,* late twentieth-century humans seem to be constantly and desperately hoping that there is a 'plan' to existence, and that our otherwise senseless actions can be tied together in a teleologically meaningful way. Godot never comes in Beckett's play. But deep inside us, as audience members, we yearningly hope that Beckett is wrong, and that on some other stage, in some other play, the design of things will become known to us – that Godot will indeed come. This is the dilemma, the contingent emotional plight that is nowadays commonly called post-modern. It is not the purpose here to define or discuss this much debated and studied condition of the contemporary human psyche. Suffice it to say that it is typical of industrialized and urbanized individuals to be able to 'step outside' traditions and value systems and see them as concoctions of human beings, rather than as the results of inevitable historical processes. To the post-modern mind, nothing is universal; everything is relative.

In the eighteenth century, the dizzying growth of technology and the constantly increasing certainty that science could eventually solve all human problems – perhaps even prolong life indefinitely by discovering the 'life principle' and thus conquering death – brought into existence a new form of mentality. By the end of this century, the now famous assertion that 'God is dead' by the great German philosopher Friedrich Nietzsche (1844–1900) acknowledged both that the modern mind had run its course and that a new world-view had crystallized – a world-view that had lost its belief in anything beyond the immediate material form of existence.

The term post-modernism comes out of the field of architecture where it was used to describe the eclectic, colourful variety of building styles designed by urban architects in the seventies. Immediately after it was coined, the term caught on like wildfire, and is now used to describe everything from contemporary paintings to the methods of computer-influenced cognitive science. As the philosopher John Searle has recently remarked (1992: 5–6), post-modernism has produced many of the currently fashionable, but implausible, materialistic views in philosophy: for example, the idea that the mind does not exist at all; the notion that mental states are no more than causal relations between inputs and outputs of the system (organic or inorganic) of which they are a part; the view that a computer has a mind; the view that consciousness as inner reality does not exist. Contemporary intellectual culture seems to be afflicted by a kind of 'ironic' imagination – a state of mind that has led to perverse philosophies, such as those listed by Searle, as we continue, *ironically*, to search for meaning to life.

In my view there is no doubt that the contemporary version of the post-modern mind has been in large part fostered by our television-mediated culture. Viewing the world through a television camera leads to a perspective that Solomon (1988: 212) aptly characterizes as 'perceptual montage.' We gaze upon the world as if it were a television program or a scene in a television commercial. Day in and day out these fragmented images of life influence our overall view that reality is illusory. Ultimately, we are led to form the view that human actions are a montage of nonsensical skits, docudramas, commercials, and so on.

Language in the post-modern mind takes on a new modality of representation. Post-modern language is either imbued with irony or else it is reduced to mere formulas, stock phrases, and the kind of babble that television situation comedies constantly blurt out. The music that the post-modern ear hears is the senseless sounds strung together randomly by a John Cage. The art that defines the post-modern eye is that of an Andy Warhol. The post-modern mind sees no meaning in the world beyond the satisfaction of immediate survival urges and drives, and therefore finds any search for meaning as itself *meaningless*. The post-modern mind is ahistorical and nihilistic. As the sociologist Zygmunt Bauman (1992: vii–viii) has perceptively remarked, post-modernism is 'a state of mind marked above all by its all-deriding, all-eroding, all-dissolving *destructiveness*.'

How did this all come about? Nietzsche's nihilistic statement that 'God is dead' means, of course, that everything in human belief systems, including religious beliefs, is a construction of the human mind. By the early part of the twentieth century the view that history had a purpose which was 'narrated,' so to speak, by a divine source (as, for example, in the Bible) was coming increasingly under attack. At mid century, Western society was starting to become increasingly more 'deconstructive,' in other words, more inclined to take apart the structures – moral, social, and mental – that had been shaped by this narrative. By the sixties, Western society had become fully entangled in a post-modern frame of mind. The results have been quite noticeable in the contemporary teenager. Today, an increasingly larger group of teenagers lives outside the traditional moral structures and value systems of the culture, without a sense of purpose above and beyond the immediacy of the moment. This is reflected in the music of bands such as Guns N' Roses, which depicts scenes of drug addiction, suicide, and hate mongering. Demonic imagery is becoming more and more typical, as rock bands like Motley Crüe and Death Metal attract a small, but not insignificant, group of followers.

Now, I must re-emphasize that not every teenager in our culture thinks and behaves in this way. There are many who, as a matter of fact, react vehemently against this kind of outlook. But it is becoming symptomatic of increasingly larger sectors of the teen population. The post-modern teenager will tend to belong to a clique with its own models of behaviour and its own value systems. This entails specific codes of dress, hairstyle, bodily demeanour, language, and general comportment. Musical styles, and the performers associated with them, often dictate even the name with which a clique is known (punk rockers, hard rockers, housers, rappers, etc.). Gone are the mythic rock heroes à la Elvis Presley or à la the Beatles. Allegiance to the clique is the primary motivation that guides the post-modern teenager's daily life. As in Alexandre Dumas's 1844 novel *The Three Musketeers*, the philosophy of the clique has become 'all for one, one for all.' The post-modern teenager reflects a kind of radical response to the disenchantment with the traditional moral codes and models of our culture. No wonder, then, that *coolness*, in any of its versions, has become such a compelling, widespread behavioural phenomenon. Like never before, the teenager of today is projected into a confused, often violent and dangerous, subculture that all too frequently extols destructiveness. Becoming cool allows him or her to cope within this subculture.

It has become abundantly clear to me that understanding how teenagers think and behave has become crucial for charting the future course of our social and moral traditions. My decade-long work with teenagers has made it obvious to me that the best access route to how the contemporary teenager thinks is through the symbology of *coolness*. The objective of the next two chapters is, therefore, to paint a semiotic portrait of this deeply rooted feature of the teenage persona.

# 2

# The Emergence of Coolness

*Physical attractiveness has an important relationship to the adolescent's positive self-evaluation, popularity, and peer acceptance. Physical attractiveness is an important ingredient in interpersonal attraction. It influences personality development, social relationships, and social behaviour.*
Rice (1990: 148)

The symbolic and behavioural feature that distinguishes teenagerhood is *coolness*. The expression *cool* comes out of the jazz club scene of the 1930s (Thorne 1990: 107). When the air in the smoke-filled nightclubs of that era became unbreathable, windows and doors were opened to allow some 'cool air' in from the outside to help clear away the suffocating air. By analogy, the slow and smooth jazz style that was typical of that late-night scene came to be called 'cool.' *Cool* was subsequently extended to describe any physically attractive, male jazz musician or aficionado who patronized such clubs. Recently, the makers of Camel's cigarettes have strategically revived the nightclub coolness theme in their magazine ads and billboards. In one ad, a camel, dressed in a 'nightclubbish' white jacket, is enjoying the cool breeze coming in off the seashore. A cigarette is placed gingerly between his lips, dangling suggestively from the side of his mouth. He holds a rose in his hand, a symbol of love. He's obviously 'making eyes' at someone. The camel conveys an image of total coolness, recalling the socialite smoothness and finesse embodied by thirties and forties cinema stars, especially Humphrey Bogart in *Casablanca*.

Coolness entails a set of specific behavioural characteristics that vary in detail from generation to generation, from clique to clique, but which retain a common essence. It is firmly anchored in a *symbology* – a set of discernible bodily movements, postures, facial expressions, voice modulations, and so on – that is acquired, and takes on strategic social value, within the peer context. First and foremost, coolness implies a deliberately slow and lackadaisical form of bodily locomotion, accompanied by a nonchalant and unflappable countenance. One is never to be seen in a state of hurriedness, embarrassment, or timidity. The walk is laggard, to the point of being a saunter or a stroll. The head is always tilting or gyrating in a deliberately slow, semicircular motion. The face is unperturbed, unexcited, composed. The cool teen never shows any intense emotion. Being cool involves a control over emotionally induced body states. Losing one's cool, as the expression goes, is to be avoided at all costs. Coolness includes a cautious, purposeful avoidance of emotional outbursts, and an ability to disguise or camouflage behaviours perceived to be clumsy, awkward, inept, and, above all else, embarrassing.

The sum and substance of coolness is a self-conscious aplomb in overall behaviour. Nothing can upset a cool teen. Everything he or she does unfolds in slow motion, with self-assurance and self-confidence. In the fifties, the expression *cool cat* was often used to describe a socially attractive male teen. The metaphor of the cat is an appropriate one. A cat's languid, sleek, measured movements have the bodily rhythms and modulations that coolness wants to evoke. The deliberate slackening of one's comportment includes an attenuation of voice inflection and rate of speech. In the fifties 'cool talk' by male teens was modelled after Elvis's Southern drawl. In the sixties it became more 'Liverpoolish-sounding,' after the Beatles. Today, it varies from a kind of 'stoned out' Cheech and Chong drawl – a form of verbal delivery giving the impression that the speaker is slightly 'wasted' or 'stoned out' on drugs or alcohol, in imitation of the speech patterns used by the actors Cheech and Chong in their seventies and eighties drug movies – to the 'surfer language' used in movies and television shows.

Coolness also entails specific dress codes, hairstyles, and *modi vivendi*. The cool male teenager of the fifties, for instance, wore his hair in imitation of Elvis Presley's sideburn hairstyle, owned a car, smoked cigarettes, and donned black trousers which were tight at the ankles. An example of this cool teen was embodied in the television character known as 'The Fonz' on the seventies sitcom 'Happy Days.' Today, there are many models of coolness for males and females to follow, many of which are unisex. Wearing baseball caps pointing backwards, baggy pants, ultra long-sleeve shirts and jackets, and unlaced running shoes, for instance, are features of the early nineties symbology of coolness.

A caveat is in order at this point. When talking about the teenage subculture, it is easy to fall into the trap of overgeneralizing. Needless to say, not all teenagers aspire to become cool. Moreover, coolness is no longer homogeneous in form. It is now largely acquired and ensconced in clique settings, and therefore quite heterogeneous. Some specific cliques within the teen subculture, like *punk rockers* or *Mods*, even make it their primary goal to set themselves apart from the version of coolness described at the end of the previous paragraph. Their clothing styles, language, hairstyles, and body language often are intended to be in stark opposition to the 'slack' form of coolness. Therefore, it is probably more accurate to say that there exist *general* and *specific* models of coolness within the contemporary teenage subculture. Punk rockers and Mods no doubt consider themselves to be cool in their own particular way. Coolness is a perceived state to which many (if not most) teens now aspire, even if its specific behavioural forms can vary substantially; and if teens do not aspire to coolness, they can certainly recognize its manifestations in their peers. In a recent study of teenage language, Teresa Labov (1992) found, in fact, that the word *cool*, and what it connotes, is known by virtually everyone in the North American teen subculture, no matter what class, ethnic community, region, and so on, from which he or she comes.

Coolness can be said to form a continuum, which ranges from an extreme form of 'slack coolness' at one end to an extreme form of 'rough coolness' at the other. Punk rockers, then, would be located at the rough end, exemplifying aggressive behaviour, vulgar language, and so forth. Most teens, however, develop an average, or mid-continuum, form of coolness. But no matter where a teenager falls on the continuum, coolness has now become a fact of teen life in consumer society. It is the inevitable end-product of what Erving Goffman (1959: 208) has called 'impression management.' This is a social strategy that involves the skilful deployment of 'attributes that are required of a performer for the work of successfully staging a character.' The cool teen is indeed a 'staged character,' an individual who is highly capable of managing and manipulating the symbolic order (facial expression, dress code, mannerisms, etc.) to impress his or her peers.

Although perceptions of what constitutes coolness within mainstream teen subculture are now heterogeneous and subject to rapid change, on the basis of my own observations of teenagers over a decade, I believe the essential features of coolness have not changed drastically since the fifties. The 'average' cool teen still smokes cigarettes, walks and speaks lethargically, wears the 'right' clothes, and assumes postures deemed to be acceptable and desirable by his or her peers.

But there are some differences worthy of note. In the fifties coolness was a behavioural state to which only some male teens aspired. Salinger's Stradlater was the first portrait in fiction of male teen coolness and the 'Stradlaters' of the fifties were raised to the level of godlike heroes by their peers. They were both feared and venerated for their perceived physical and sexual prowess; and their presence at parties was much sought after. By the late sixties, the desire and need to be cool was felt even more intensely throughout the teen subculture. Coolness also became less and less the exclusive domain of male teens. By the seventies and eighties, more and more female teens started to smoke openly, and to walk and act slowly and lackadaisically; but, at the same time, they differed from their male counterparts in specific aspects of coolness. In the next chapter I will illustrate how gender coding manifests itself in the semiotics of smoking. Suffice it to say here that among both male and female teens coolness has become a synonym for social attractiveness, and its opposite, *loserness*, has become a synonym for ugliness and alienation.

The categories of *firstness*, *secondness*, and *thirdness*, posited by the American philosopher, mathematician, and semiotician Charles S. Peirce (1958), can be enlisted at this point to shed psychological light on the emergence of coolness during teenagerhood. In the area of human mental growth, *firstness* refers to an initial mind-world in the developing child that is based on a direct sensory experience of reality. The child employs this form of mentality to differentiate his or her inner world from the outer world of objects, beings, and events. This explains why the single most characteristic feature of infancy is the symbolic construction of the self – the 'I,' the psychic 'first person.' *Secondness* is the stage during which an awareness of a 'second,' or 'other,' crystallizes in human mentality. The emergence of socially dominated cognition at puberty is a consequence of secondness. *Thirdness* characterizes the adult's mind-world, the world of reflective, 'objective' thinking. The ability to separate the self abstractly from world events and from the life experiences of others is a feature of mental thirdness. According to Piagetian psychology, thirdness should emerge around the age of puberty. However, there is little doubt in my mind that contemporary teenagerhood has brought about a prolonged period of secondness. Early teenagerhood in particular unfolds primarily within the confines of a secondness mind-world, a world regulated and shaped by a 'self-other' form of consciousness.

In this chapter I will look at how coolness, as a general behavioural trait of teenagerhood, is acquired through the process of *signifying osmosis*, and how it is tied to body image and the emergence of socially based cognition (secondness). I will conclude by discussing how the quest to become cool now entails clique membership as well as regular participation at parties. My descriptions and commentaries are based primarily on my observations of, and interactions with, adolescents during the ten-year period I dedicated to studying the semiotics of teen behaviour as it unfolded naturally in contexts where teens were likely to intermingle (in school yards, at parties, in shopping malls, etc.).

### Signifying Osmosis

Puberty induces noticeable changes in physical appearance. In our culture it is not unusual for teens to find the emotional changes that accompany the physical ones traumatic. This is why teenagers tend to become inordinately concerned about their appearance and behaviour, and to believe that everyone is constantly observing them (Erikson 1950, 1968; Elkind 1967, 1984, 1988; Buis and Thompson 1989). Howard Gardner (1982: 567–8) offers the following insightful assessment of teenage secondness:

Because they are increasingly preoccupied with self-development, adolescents are typically concerned with nearly every facet – be it handwriting, clothing, or nicknames – of their own person. These trivial but telling details function as personal statement, determining how adolescents define themselves and how the community defines them. And because adolescents have an unstable image of themselves, they are concerned about how they are regarded by others in their society.

To deflect the criticism of peers away from themselves, teenagers typically deploy several defensive strategies. For example, they often talk in a caustic and sarcastic manner about how others act, behave, and appear. The words they are constantly coining to describe other teens – *geek, nerd, doorknob, shithead,* and so on – are generally intended to be derogatory. Conformity in dress and hairstyle is another safeguard that teens employ in order to divert critical attention away from themselves. Above all else, the desire to become cool constitutes a defensive behavioural strategy – a strategy designed to transform the physiological and emotional changes that occur at puberty into peer-shaped and peer-acceptable patterns of social behaviour.

During childhood the human being's modes of interaction with the environment and with others centre on a constantly developing consciousness of self. The child is typically concerned with learning about how the self fits into the scheme of things. At puberty, however, the child's consciousness becomes progressively more sensitive to the presence of others. Social cognition soon begins to dominate his or her thinking and actions. While human beings of all ages are influenced by the opinions of others, and tend to conform to behavioural models acceptable to their peer groups, teenagers are particularly susceptible to peer influence simply because social cognition emerges in their lives as a powerful new form of thought. The cliquing phenomenon, for instance, is a manifestation of the power of social cognition over behaviour during adolescence.

There is nothing particularly unique about teenage peer bonding, or the capacity of juveniles to form close, symmetrical relations. The phenomenon of 'psycho-attachment'(Keesing 1981: 19) – the predisposition to form social bonds with other individuals in the life cycle – is part of the genetic heritage of all primates. Peer bonding is a crucial 'mechanism in maintaining solidarity and reducing conflict within the group' (19). Perhaps what sets modern humans apart from their primate relatives is the fact that they no longer have to leave the natal group at puberty. Among chimpanzees, the female adolescent voluntarily leaves the natal group shortly after puberty to find a community in which to mate. Both male and female adolescent gibbons, who live in small, monogamous family communities, emigrate at puberty. And if they don't leave voluntarily, they are ejected from the group. Examples of the emigration of primates at puberty are bountiful. As Steinberg (1987: 38–9) suggests, if taken together the primate studies indicate that it is advantageous from the standpoint of reproductive fitness to leave the natal group at adolescence. Mating within the group would threaten the species' gene pool. It can therefore be suggested that by prolonging the mating period we have *ipso facto* created the conditions conducive to the emergence of teenager-hood in our culture. The cool behaviours contemporary teenagers regularly exhibit are explainable as probable reflexes of repressed mating tendencies seeking an outlet.

Given that teenagerhood is a cultural construction, the question now becomes: How does the pubescent adolescent become a *teenager*, a new social being displaying a specific form of behaviour known as coolness? In the previous chapter I suggested that the formation of the teenage persona is the result of a process that can be called *signifying osmosis*. This term requires some elaboration.

*Osmosis* is used to describe the process by which something is acquired by absorption. In organisms, osmosis can be understood as the largely unconscious tendency to assimilate or absorb the behavioural mannerisms of other organisms within the immediate environment. The human organism is biologically predisposed to acquire sense-based and affectively meaningful forms of behaviour osmotically. The philosopher Susanne Langer (1948) convincingly argued that, at a primary level of mind, we apprehend the world through 'feeling'; in other words, we tend to 'feel' first that the world has a structure. She called this the 'presentational' form of cognition. It is only at a later stage that we tend to conceptualize and verbalize our feeling-states, giving them a more 'understandable,' logical form. She referred to this as the 'discursive' form of cognition. Recent discussions on the presence of feeling in thought have come forward to support Langer's insights. Gendlin (1991), for instance, suggests that bodily sensation is present in all thinking in such a way that it is even more 'ordered' than language and logic. Johnson (1991) has gone so far as to claim that all linguistic and logical categories are derivatives of bodily experience. The point to be made here is that presentational forms of behaviour are acquired osmotically: that is, they are assimilated at first in a largely unconscious manner, especially if the behaviour in question is felt to be socially meaningful or advantageous. The bodily postures, facial expressions, modes of dress, and discourse features that characterize social behaviour in general can be seen to result from this tendency.

The assimilation of certain behaviours can also result from mimesis. *Mimesis* can be defined simply as conscious osmosis. It is the tendency of human beings to imitate certain behaviours in order to acquire them, especially if they are perceived to be desirable or socially advantageous.

*Signifying osmosis* is a term referring to the osmotic assimilation of behaviour as it unfolds in relation to socially meaningful, or *signifying*, stimuli. In my view, signifying osmosis is responsible for many of the bodily movements, postures, facial expressions, discourse features, and so on, that teens acquire through peer contact (see also Bandura and Walters 1959, and McDonald 1977 on this point). This process is at the basis of *communal signification* (or meaning-making) within the peer group.

Recently, an interesting, though unfounded, theory has been put forward which claims that ultimately all ideas and styles (dress, musical, etc.) develop a kind of mimetic life of their own. The sociobiologist Richard Dawkins (1976, 1987) has argued rather persuasively that mimesis is responsible for the transmission and entrenchment of concepts and behaviours within specific cultural settings. He calls transmitted ideas or styles *memes*, in direct imitation of the word *genes*. Dawkins defines *memes* simply as replicating patterns of information (tunes, ideas, clothing fashions, etc.).

Dawkins's idea of memes captures rather nicely how the forms of behaviour that teens pick up through direct contact with each other tend to develop a life of their own. But meme theory would not explain the clique-coded variations in behavioural symbology that teens constantly manifest. Behavioural models are not acquired *at first* via mimesis, but rather via signifying osmosis. It is only at a later stage that these are reinforced, generalized, and spread through media mimesis and through the commercial diffusion of products such as videos and records. The rock music channel MTV, which is now seen in many countries, has become a source for the mimetic spread abroad of North American teen models of behaviour – models that have, however, an osmotic origin.

## Body Image

It is appropriate to start off a semiotic analysis of coolness with a consideration of body image, given that the advent of semiotics coincided with the advent of medicine in antiquity. As a science of signs, including bodily symptoms, semiotics grew out of attempts by the first Western physicians to understand how the association of bodily states with diseases was forged within specific cultural domains. Indeed, in its oldest usage, the term *semeiotica* was applied to the study of physiological symptoms induced by particular diseases. Hippocrates (460?–377? BC) – the founder of medical science – viewed the ways in which an individual in a specific cultural setting would perceive and relate the symptoms associated with a disease as the basis for making an appropriate diagnosis and formulating a suitable prognosis. The physician Galen of Pergamum (AD 130?– 200?) similarly argued that successful diagnosis was dependent not only on an examination of bodily symptoms, but also on an understanding of the culture-specific perceptions associated with those symptoms. In Italy, the term semeiotica continues, in fact, to be used in medical science to refer to the study of symptoms. It was soon after Hippocrates' use of the term *semeion* to refer to the culture-specific representation of a symptom that it came to mean, by the time of Aristotle (384–22 BC), a *sign* in general. So, from early times to the present age, it has always been recognized within Western culture – at least implicitly – that there is an intrinsic connection between the body, the mind, and culture, and that the process that links these three dimensions of human existence is *semiosis*, the production and interpretation of signs.

The human body is a source of signification. The emergence of a heightened sensitivity to the body as an imparter of meaning indicates that secondness, or social cognition, has taken hold of the child's developmental process. When children become excessively concerned about their physical appearance, then from a social standpoint they have, in effect, become teenagers, even if they have not yet become pubescent. Indeed, the onset of teenagerhood is no longer coincident with adolescence (the advent of puberty). Pre-pubescent children frequently manifest many symbological features of teenagerhood. Childhood has been abbreviated considerably since the mid fifties. It is not unusual today to find eight- or nine-year-olds who look, think, and act like teenagers.

The first sign that sensitivity to body image has emerged in the child is an acute preoccupation with body size – slim vs. fat, tall vs. short, and so on. This preoccupation indicates that signifying osmotic processes in the child have been activated. The association of slimness with attractiveness, for instance, which is reinforced through media models, is initially acquired through contact with teens. Teens tend to ostracize 'fat' peers from their social milieu and activities. This intersection of media mimesis with signifying osmosis turns body size for the 'new teen' – often called a *teeny-bopper* – into an issue of high moral, social, and aesthetic value.

The preparation and *presentation* of the body, to use a term suggested by Erving Goffman (1959), is a social strategy designed to secure peer approbation. This is why the inability to present a peer-acceptable body image, or why even the belief that one's body is socially undesirable, can have dire consequences. The increase since the fifties in eating disorders such as anorexia nervosa and bulimia among female teenagers is frightening (Bruch 1978; Brumberg 1988; Manley 1989; Yates 1989, 1990). The presentation of self has clearly become enormously problematic within the teenage subculture. For the modern teen, the 'body is as much symbol as substance,' as Averill (1990: 117) aptly puts it. In the contemporary teen subculture, and in society generally, the slim and lean look is a prerequisite for attaining coolness for both males and females. The margin of flexibility for deviating from this idealized body type is larger for males than it is for females; instead males must strive to develop a muscular look.

For female teens, the size of their breasts also constitutes a problem of body image. Teenage girls are very concerned about their breasts being either too big or too small. The same kind of sensitivity is felt by their male counterparts vis-à-vis penis size, with the general principle being 'the bigger, the more masculine.' As Crook (1991: 13) has remarked, this sensitivity to idealized body prototypes causes teens to become permanently discontented with their appearance:

Most teens still believe that they are the only ones who don't fit, who have a dumpy body, who are awkward, ugly, fat. If they are part of a social group that emphasizes sports or theater or just one that does not overemphasize 'looking good,' such humiliation is only an occasional burden ... But many teens socialize with other teens who think 'looking good' is the only worthwhile goal and who practice small cruelties on teens who do not measure up to their standards.

As I was conducting research on teen behaviour several years ago, I occasionally had the opportunity to observe firsthand the nature of the 'small cruelties' of which Crook speaks. These ranged all the way from name-calling incidents ('Hey, fatso!' 'Looks like a tanker trailer rolled in today!') to actual acts of physical aggression perpetrated against anyone who didn't fit the prescribed models of slimness.

To enhance body image, teens typically resort to various forms of decoration and camouflage. In general, they attempt to hide or masquerade all facial blemishes and flaws such as pimples and oversized organs (nose and ears). The wearing of eyeglasses is perceived to detract from a cool appearance. Only dorks and losers wear them. In the case of female teens, facial hair is considered to be particularly undesirable; male teens, on the other hand, perceive beard growth as enhancing their masculine coolness. Once again, it must be emphasized that the teens in some cliques attempt to shatter such models of coolness by decorating their body intentionally in 'ugly' ways, by letting their facial hair grow, by highlighting their ugly features through cosmetic emphasis, and so on. The ideal body image can be found at more than one position on the 'coolness continuum.'

Underlying the preoccupation with body image is, of course, the emergence of sexual feelings. *Making out* (engaging in sexual activity) is available only to those who fit peer-sanctioned models of bodily attractiveness. Needless to say, our perceptions of what is gender-appropriate sexuality are susceptible to cultural shaping. Humans the world over can literally 'sense' and 'model' the essence of 'maleness' and 'femaleness': that is, humans, like other animals, can sense and feel differences in *sex*. This ability is tied to the organism's reactions to signals in the environment and to urges within itself. To use Langer's (1948) theory of cognition once again, these reactions are 'presentational' at first. Subsequently, they are 'represented' (literally 'presented again') in terms of culturally coded models. In fact, it is only when presentational models of 'maleness' and 'femaleness' are represented culturally that conceptualizations of *masculinity* and *femininity* respectively are forged, conventionalized, and institutionalized.

Consider the concept of *love*, the dominant theme of rock ballads from the fifties onwards. The origin of this concept is to be found in instinctive responses such as an increase in blood flow, muscle tension, salivation, and so on, which are registered presentationally as memorable feeling-states. At this level, 'love' is an affective state. Through cultural sense-making, some of the constituents of this state are then connected metaphorically to each other to form the concept *love*. At this higher level love can be thought of, for example, as a gustatory reaction: 'You're so sweet, She's my sweetheart,' and so forth. The transformational process has now been completed: 'love' has been transferred from the world of feeling-states to the world of conceptualization (see Kövecses 1986, 1988, 1990 for a similar view of concept formation). It is interesting to note that once a concept has been formed in this way it can then be extended to cultural institutions and behaviours. Rituals of love making in our culture, as a matter of fact, normally involve the 'love is sweet' concept: for example, sweets are given to a loved one at St Valentine's day, matrimonial love is symbolized at a wedding ceremony by the eating of a cake, and so on.

The sexual basis of body image in teenagerhood leads to gender-coded differences in the ways in which teenagers prepare and present their bodies for peer spectators. The differences that I was able to document from my research forays are compatible with the general findings in this domain (e.g., Glass 1992: 46–8). These included the following dichotomies:

| Male Teens | Female Teens |
|---|---|
| They tend to take up more space when sitting, standing, etc. | They generally occupy less space in comparable situations. |
| Their movements tend to be more angular, rigid, and restricted in range. | Their movements, on the other hand, are inclined to be more fluid, sleek, and deliberate. |
| They invade other people's body space more often. | They are less likely to invade the body space of others. |
| They are more unlikely to touch others. | They are more inclined to touch both male and female peers. |
| They are inclined to fidget and shift bodily positions more often. | They are less inclined to fidget and shift bodily positions. |
| They move around more when talking. | They are more stationary when talking. |

An intriguing study by Mary Jenni in 1976 showed how body consciousness entails gender-coded behavioural comportment even in the ways in which individuals carry their books. Specifically, she found that the females coming from and going into a library tended to clasp books against their bodies with one or both arms wrapped around the books, whereas the males almost always carried their books in one hand at the side of their bodies.

This example of unconscious gender-coded bodily behaviour is, in my view, explainable in terms of signifying osmosis: that is, it is acquired through contact with peers in socially meaningful contexts. As Gardner (1982: 545) aptly puts it, such findings 'illustrate the powerful influence and interplay of biological and social factors in determining patterns of behaviour.'

There is one last observation to be made about teen body image that falls under the category of *proxemics* – the branch of semiotics that studies the symbolic structure of the physical space maintained between bodies in social contexts. Edward T. Hall's (1966) often quoted study of the proxemic organization of physical space is relevant to the present discussion. Hall noted that the dimensions of the invisible boundary people maintained when interacting could be measured very accurately, allowing for predictable statistical variation, and that the boundary dimensions varied from culture to culture. In North American culture, for instance, he discovered that a distance of less than six inches between two people was perceived to be an 'intimate' distance; he measured the acceptable 'social' distance at from four to twelve feet. He found, moreover, that overstepping a boundary causes considerable discomfort. If a stranger were to talk at a distance of only several centimetres away from someone, he or she would be considered rude or even aggressive. If the 'safe' distance is breached by an acquaintance, on the other hand, it would probably be interpreted as a sexual advance.

The proxemic organization of physical space plays a

prominent role in teen body presentation. Conscious of body odours, facial imperfections, and the like, teens are more likely to stay well beyond the boundary limits set by North American culture generally. Intrusions occur primarily in the context of clique gatherings and intimate settings such as parties. In the latter context, however, the lighting is kept low and the music is played loudly in part to deflect attention away from bodily imperfections, even though such choreographic strategies are designed primarily to emphasize the sexual nature of the event. The use of body image enhancers, such as perfumes, is common at parties for the same reason.

The last statement requires some elaboration. Perfume is an artificial extension of the body's odour-producing system. At the biological level, humans, like other animals, are responsive to odours and scents that are emitted by others. Certain body odours function as sexual stimulants. Although the sense of sight has largely replaced the sense of smell as a means of sexual arousal in humans – modern humans are more inclined to respond to erotic images than to bodily smells – the need to involve the olfactory system sexually at a more basic level has not disappeared completely from our species.

Semiotically, perfume is a surrogate for sexually meaningful scent. It is designed to work on the sexual emotions and is therefore quite apt to make a long-lasting impression. Years after an infatuation we seldom fail to recognize a fragrance that was worn by a loved one. A scent can bring vividly to mind a past situation and reawaken the corresponding feelings associated with it (Engen 1982: 13). Odours are also associated with meaningful spaces and places. We prefer the familiar 'smell of home' to that of other abodes. We react negatively to the smell of places such as dental offices where we might have had unpleasant experiences. So, teens wear perfumes not only to hide body odours, but also, unconsciously, to 'replace' them with artificial enhancers of sexual attractiveness.

## Social Cognition

*Social cognition* can be defined as 'how people think about other people and about themselves, or how people come to know their social world' (Rice 1990: 105). The emergence of a heightened sense of social cognition, or secondness, as puberty approaches leads the adolescent to construct a theory of the self in relation to others (Okun and Sasfy 1977: 378). Elkind (1971: 11) has put it in the following words:

During adolescence the young person develops a true 'sense of self.' While children are aware of themselves, they are not able to put themselves in other people's shoes and to look at themselves from that perspective. Adolescents can do this and do engage in such self-watching to a considerable extent. Indeed, the characteristic 'self-consciousness' of the adolescent results from the very fact that the young person is now very much concerned with how others react to him. This is a concern that is largely absent in childhood.

In this state of mind, adolescents will go to great lengths to protect their vulnerable identity. This is why a teenager will typically transform his or her bedroom into a haven for protecting and sheltering the self. Bedrooms seem to be particularly meaningful places and concealing a bedroom has a biological basis. We are extremely vulnerable when we are sleeping, and so it is judicious to keep sleeping areas hidden or secret. The ancient Egyptians concealed their bedrooms at the back or the sides of their homes. North American families also prefer to keep their bedrooms out of sight.

An adolescent will guard access to his or her bedroom with fanatical zeal. In this private space the adolescent unwinds, relaxes, and defines his or her symbolic universe through decoration (posters, photos), sounds (stereo equipment with appropriate tapes, compact discs, etc.), and tokens of peer friendship (gifts, memorabilia, letters, etc.). The bedroom is a sacred space for the adolescent, a refuge and asylum from the world. Here no one is looking at his or her imperfections. Only 'intimates' are allowed to share that space symbolically. All other visitations are felt to be annoying intrusions (including parents who enter the room to clean it themselves or to instruct their adolescent son or daughter to clean it). But even within the private world of the bedroom, teens feel the need to keep continually in contact with their peers. For this reason, the telephone is perceived as a crucial 'pipeline' to other peers. This is why, given the increasing economic feasibility of owning a phone, the contemporary teen will typically demand to have his or her own private phone. He or she will use it primarily as a means for keeping in touch with peers, for recounting events of importance to their social life, and for organizing social events.

Of course, not all teens have a private bedroom or phone. In many households the bedroom is shared, by necessity, with others. But, it is accurate to say that most teens at least desire their own private space and phone, whether or not these are obtainable.

The onset of social cognition at puberty, as mentioned above, entails the deployment of defensive strategies designed to deflect attention away from oneself. One such strategy is humour. So-called dirty jokes hide a preoccupation with sexuality; jokes bragging about failure at school reflect anxiety over academic performance; jokes about the appearance of others indicate a deeply felt need to hide perceived imperfections in the presentation of self by deflecting peer criticism towards others. Irony in particular emerges at puberty as a powerful defensive verbal strategy. The ability to construct ironic verbal texts allows the adolescent to confront problems and to present the self in tactful ways. These texts, as Gardner (1982: 539) aptly

points out, are means of combining 'aggressive and sexual
themes with wordplay in a presentation that conveys self
as well as story.'

## The Cliquing Phenomenon

Today, the need to secure membership in a clique is felt
strongly by most teens and pre-teens. Cliques have the
protective function within the high school (and even
junior high school) context of drawing together specific
teens and of keeping outsiders out. A teen will tend to seek
membership in a clique that provides opportunities for
status achievement and coolness that are compatible with
his or her natural abilities, attributes, or preferences: for
example, a physically powerful teen will tend to join a
clique that perceives physical aggression as prestigious.
The high school community, therefore, exemplifies a
small-scale model of status achievement. Status is configured symbolically by specific traits. The person most
likely to climb the teen status scale is the one best able to
manipulate the shared symbols of status and power in the
high school setting. As Lenski (1966: 57) has put it, 'power
and status are achieved through the ability to manipulate
the social situation of others.' And, according to Doherty
(1988: 98), cliques are of the utmost importance to a teenager's life because they provide him or her with emotional
shelter and a means for establishing and reinforcing 'presence, identity, and solidarity.' As Ausubel, Montemayor,
and Svajian (1977: 334) have written, cliques undergird
'the *structure* of norms in the school from which all actions
performed by students result.'

Musical preferences also influence clique selection. This
is why cliques are often named after rock styles, genres, or
bands. During my field work I discovered that the following clique names were in vogue during the late eighties,
and some of them still continue to be used as I write:

- Housers: The members of this clique assigned great

value to house music and to the dance club scene connected with it.

- Rockers (also called *hard rockers, metalloyds,* or *metallurgists*): This was the name employed to identify those who listened to hard rock bands, including such late sixties and seventies bands as Pink Floyd, Led Zeppelin, and The Doors. Knowing the songs of hard rock groups, and wearing the apparel that band members wore (leather boots, ripped jeans, leather jackets, etc.), were seen to be among the primary requirements for clique membership in the rockers.

- Mods: These teens listened to the new wave music of the mid eighties and were generally sympathetic to the punk rock movement.

- Ginos and Ginas: This is how those teens who stayed together on the basis of ethnic heritage were referred to. Ginos and Ginas typically came from Italian households, wore stylish clothing, and listened to disco-type music.

- Bat Cavers: This was the name used to identify those teens who were *Rocky Horror Picture Show* aficionados and wore gothic-style black clothes in imitation of the costumes worn by the movie's actors and actresses.

- Dead Heads: Teens who listened to sixties music and who wore hippie-style clothing were called Dead Heads. The name was derived from the sixties rock group The Grateful Dead.

- B-Boys: This was the name used to characterize those teens who wore baseball jackets and caps and who listened to rap music.

- Normals (or Norms): Any teen who did not belong to a

clique with specific musical, clothing, and grooming requirements was a Norm. Nevertheless, Norms were still perceived to constitute an identifiable ensemble by virtue of the fact that they did not belong to one of the other cliques and by virtue of the fact that they often congregated in a clique-like manner at social events.

There is nothing especially innovative about this kind of terminology, whose aim it is to define a clique metonymically, in terms of a single attribute. In a 1978 study, for example, Leona reported that the general student population in Boston high schools had special names for members of various cliques. These included *jocks*, or teenagers actively involved in sports, *motorheads*, who spent most of their time driving or repairing cars, and *fleabags*, who consumed drugs. Teenagers who do not belong to a clique risk being ostracized and being labelled *losers* by their more socially inclined peers. Losers are adolescents who do not possess, or aspire to possess, any of the critical attributes for clique membership and, therefore, of coolness. They do not perceive the high school environment as a locus for socialization, and, as a consequence, risk being ridiculed by their cool peers. They are the ones who are commonly referred to nowadays with such derogatory epithets as *dorks*, *geeks*, and *nerds* (Danesi 1989a). Such names, incidentally, abound in the teen lexicon. Labov (1992: 360) has documented the main ones that were used in the late eighties by teens throughout North America to describe certain personality types. These reveal the wide range of personalities that teens perceive their peers to have:

*jocks, rednecks, nerds, dweebs, rah-rahs, motor heads, freaks, squids, airheads, myrons, douche bags, druggies, dudes, dexters, fleabags, mondos, geeks, potheads, homies, bougies, burn-outs, dirt balls, band fags, wimps, war pigs, punk rockers, rockers, guidos, acid heads, brains, drama fags, punks, greasers, weirdos.*

Belonging to a clique entails acquiring certain specific behavioural characteristics osmotically. A teeny-bopper who sees himself or herself as a hard rocker, for instance, will eventually develop a 'hard' personality. The hard rocker will typically manifest aggressive behaviour, utter obscenities regularly, wear ripped jeans, boots, and long hair, and listen to heavy metal music. By unconsciously modelling his or her behaviour after clique members, the teenager is really seeking to secure protection against the psychological ravages associated with what Erikson (1950) called 'identity diffusion,' a state in which teenagers feel overwhelmed by the many choices they face, including choices about gender identity. A clique constitutes a 'shelter' system, a closed social network in which the teen can immerse and hide his or her insecure and vulnerable identity. As mentioned in the previous chapter, this produces a fervent allegiance to the clique reminiscent of the oath taken by the musketeers in Alexandre Dumas's classic 1844 novel, *The Three Musketeers*: 'All for one, one for all.' This attitude can, however, expose the teenager to considerable danger, since it is undergirded by the conviction that 'bad things will happen to others, not to us.' This sense of allegiance can make a teenager feel indestructible and, therefore, oblivious to the perils inherent in the risks that clique members might require of him or her (consuming alcohol and drugs, smoking cigarettes, accepting physical challenges from a member of another clique, etc.).

There is one other facet of the cliquing phenomenon that is worthy of note here: most clique formations are ephemeral and their make up and organizational structure change over time. As Dunphy (1963) remarked a few decades ago, there is an evolutionary cycle that characterizes cliques. When a clique is formed it normally consists of young teens. Moreover, at its inception it tends to be mainly unisexual and isolated from other cliques. A little later on the clique typically starts to interact with other cliques. During subsequent stages, the clique opens itself up more and more to members of the opposite sex. Finally, heterosexual bonding occurs within the clique, signaling its disintegration.

Cliques tend to have a strong and charismatic leader. As in the case of other primate associational formations, such as baboons (e.g., Morris 1990: 24–5), power is normally invested in a dominant male in mixed-gender cliques. This arrangement, as Morris suggests, provides physical protection for the entire clique. However, among teen cliques this is not always the case. There is a growing tendency in mixed-gender cliques for a male to share power with a designated female. Usually, this entails emotional and sexual bonds between the two power brokers. But whatever the arrangement, the teenage clique invariably has a well-defined power structure.

To get a firsthand glimpse into the cliquing phenomenon, in February 1991 I visited, along with a research assistant (Christopher De Sousa), a typical suburban high school in the northwestern part of metropolitan Toronto. Twenty-five typical grade twelve students – fourteen males and eleven females – were interviewed. There was at least one representative from each of the various cliques within the school among the interviewees. The aim of the interview was to identify the features that the students perceived as crucial for defining coolness and for achieving status both within the clique and within the larger high school community. So, the subjects were asked: 'What things do you think promote coolness and status for guys and girls within your own group of friends and other groups?' The answers provided a catalogue of critical social traits:

- smoking

- quantity of alcohol consumption

- 'doing' drugs

- music preferences within the clique

- dance-related activities

- strategic use of physical aggression

- dress

- sexual promiscuity and prowess

- individuality or 'weirdness'

- academic achievement

- automobile ownership

- physical appearance

The interview made it obvious that coolness and status achievement were anchored in the symbology of appearance, peer-sanctioned physical and social behaviours, and material possessions. The interview findings are summarized below.

## Smoking

Every interviewee identified smoking cigarettes as critical for defining coolness and for gaining status within the school, for both males and females. Smoking was seen as an obligatory aspect of social behaviour at clique gatherings, especially at parties.

## Quantity of Alcohol Consumption

The consumption of alcohol in specific contexts (e.g., after school and at parties) also emerged as a desirable trait. The teens that emphasized it the most were the rockers, with the norms very close behind. Only members of the rocker clique, however, viewed alcohol consumption as a desirable attribute for both males and females. It was assigned value primarily as a male attribute by the members of all the other cliques. Thus, status achievement within the rocker and norm cliques was seen to be tied directly to the individual's ability to consume large quantities of alcohol. By the members of the other cliques, this ability was considered to be only one among other attributes of coolness.

## 'Doing' Drugs

'Doing' drugs – as the adolescents phrased it – was considered to be a cool attribute for both males and females only by the rockers. Surprisingly, it was also valued as a cool activity by the norms, but for males only. Members of the other cliques perceived it to be a relatively unimportant activity.

## Music Preferences within the Clique

As mentioned above, most of the cliques – especially the rockers, housers, and mods – derived their primary identity from a rock music style, performer, or band. Knowing the 'right' music was seen to be the critical trait for clique membership and an important one for status achievement. Norms and Ginos/Ginas claimed to have more eclectic musical preferences.

## Dance-Related Activities

This was identified as a desirable attribute for coolness and status achievement only by members of the houser clique. It was also given some importance by the members of the Ginos/Ginas clique.

## The Strategic Use of Physical Aggression

Prowess in fighting was identified as important primarily by the housers and rockers. These two cliques can be described as having a gang-like structure, and their raison d'être is perceived to be the intimidation of others. The members of houser and rocker cliques ranked skill at physical aggression and at risk taking (especially involving illegal activities) high on the coolness and status achievement scale.

## Dress

Conformity in dress was seen as a desirable attribute for both males and females by the members of all cliques except the Norms. Mods required their members to wear black clothes; rockers made the wearing of ripped, shabby jeans and cowboy-type boots mandatory; housers and Ginos/Ginas expected their members to wear stylish, expensive clothing, and so on.

## Sexual Promiscuity and Prowess

This was felt to be a critical attribute by all the interviewees, but only for males. The Norms and Ginos/Ginas, in particular, considered it a liability for females. It would seem that even among late twentieth-century teenagers, males cannot achieve social status among their peers without demonstrable sexual prowess, and that, hypocritically, females are still required to demonstrate sexual virtue!

## Individuality or 'Weirdness'

This attribute was given as desirable only by Mods. Weirdness in hairstyle, musical preference, and so on, was considered by Mods to be one of the more important attributes for both males and females for status achievement

within the clique. However, it was felt by the other interviewees to restrict status achievement within the larger
high school community.

*Academic Achievement*

Academic achievement was considered to be valuable for
status achievement primarily by female Norms and, to a
lesser extent, by male Norms. It was considered to be virtually irrelevant by all the others.

*Automobile Ownership*

This trait was identified as critical for coolness and status
achievement by only Ginos/Ginas. Indeed, in this clique it
constituted the primary requirement for moving up the
scale of status, prestige, and popularity for both males and
females.

*Physical Appearance*

The interviewees indicated that each of the cliques in their
school required specific elements of physical appearance
for membership, especially in the areas of hairstyle and
grooming.

In sum, it became clear from the interview session that
coolness was seen as a consequence of appearances, actions, and behaviours that were identified as desirable by
clique members: a Mod, for instance, would rate 'weirdness' very high on the coolness scale; a rocker, on the other
hand, would rate alcohol and drug consumption highly.
Interestingly, several of the attributes identified as critical
by the interviewees applied equally to male and female
forms of coolness. But, by and large, male teens were expected to possess more attributes than females. Status
achievement within the high school community at large –

that is, cross-clique status – seemed to be achievable for those who became particularly cool within their own clique and who, at the same time, excelled at several cross-clique attributes. Once again, it seemed that more was required of the males, especially in the areas of sexual prowess and physical aggression.

These findings are not atypical; similar ones can be found scattered throughout the research literature on adolescent cliquing behaviour. They hold a specific message for parents and educators. By knowing which clique a teenager belongs to, the parent or educator will be in a better position to know what kind of activities that teen is likely to engage in. A teen who joins a rocker-type clique, for instance, will invariably be required to consume alcohol and do drugs.

As well, it should be mentioned here that the cliquing phenomenon has been leading more and more to the formation of gangs, such as the ones formed typically by houser and rocker teens. The gang phenomenon is not new. One thinks, for instance, of the emergence of ghetto-based teen gangs in the fifties – a phenomenon, incidentally, immortalized in Leonard Bernstein's 1957 musical *West Side Story*. But the tendency to join gang-like cliques is no longer characteristic only of teens who live in inner city districts of urban centres. It has become a widespread phenomenon that cuts across all sociocultural, socio-economic, and regional lines. The reason for this, in my view, is the psychological power that the 'rough' form of coolness often has over the adolescent's world-view. Psychologists who look for the causes underlying the increase in violence among teens in the social sphere (family background, socio-economic class, etc.), or in the influence of media programs and artefacts which extol violence are, in my opinion, barking up the wrong tree. The enormous psychological power of clique symbology has probably much more to do with teen violence today than media influence or any of the traditionally accepted social causes.

Conformity to the features that define coolness within the clique, which often entail a rejection of adult models of behaviour, can have an effect on the adolescent's worldview and lifestyle for many years. Parents should not underestimate the influence that cliques can have over their adolescent's construction of models of morality and of social behaviour. Indeed, a parent can be virtually assured that his or her adolescent son or daughter has embarked on the path to maturity when he or she achieves autonomy – behavioural, emotional, and moral – from the peer group.

## Partying

There are many ways in which teens can socialize with their peers. But the desire to be involved in a party scene stands out in all surveys of teen social activities. Since the advent of the teenagerhood phenomenon in the fifties, the party scene has always been a primary locus for teen socialization. The Saturday-night party in particular – where teens can smoke, consume alcohol, tell jokes, and make sexual advances unobserved by adults – allows for the symbology of coolness to unfold in perhaps its most natural context.

The main reason the party scene has become such a common locus for socialization is that it involves the enactment of three affective states – sexuality, peer bonding, and identity construction in the peer context. Above all else, the teen party constitutes a kind of tribal mating ritual whose symbological manifestations have been captured in movies such as *Animal House* (1978), which featured teen 'party animals': young males who live for the party scene in order to 'make out' with female peers. The party is a structured performance. Acting silly and rude is expected of males, whose roles are perceived to be similar to those of clowns or *pagliacci*. Females, on the other hand, are expected to provide the sexual flirtation signals that produce the comical and exaggerated behaviours in the males – the so-called party animals.

The desire to be a part of the Saturday-night party scene is another sure sign that the child has become a teenager. Being a participant at a Saturday-night party, especially during the pre-teen and early teen years, is felt to be an important prerequisite for the development of coolness. Teens will often go to extremes of deception to hide the fact that they were not part of a Saturday-night party. Those who are forced to admit that they were not invited to a party, or that they actually preferred not to go to one, are often ostracized, derided, and even confronted physically. In later adolescence, this need is gradually attenuated as older male and female teens form sexual bonds between each other. Indeed, the transition from early teenagerhood to late adolescence is marked by the diminution of interest on the part of the individual in being a part of the Saturday-night party scene.

# 3
# An Anatomy of Coolness

*Adolescence brings about a tremendous increase in heterosexual interests and social relationships. There is little doubt that sexual attitudes and sex role behaviours are primarily shaped through peer interactions.*
Coleman and Hendry (1990: 120)

The underlying biological basis for displays of coolness is sexuality. As archaeological evidence now seems to suggest, sexually induced social behaviours have probably always been characteristic of the human species. According to Helen Fisher (1992: 272–3), Cro-Magnon adolescents apparently 'spent hours decorating themselves – as adolescents do in many cultures – plaiting their hair, donning garlands of flowers in order to smell sweet, wearing bracelets and pendants, and decorating their tunics and leggings with fur, feathers, beads, and red and yellow ocher. Then they strutted, preened, and showed off for one another around the fire's glow.'

So, the contemporary manifestations of coolness are really nothing to be alarmed about. They would seem to be linked phylogenetically to biological tendencies in the human organism – tendencies which in our age induce behavioural reflexes around puberty that are conditioned osmotically by the particular social requirements of teenagerhood. To a semiotician, coolness provides evidence of a continuity and constant dynamic interaction between the body and culture. In this chapter, I will profile precisely those behavioural reflexes – the facial expressions, dress codes, musical preferences, smoking behaviours, and 'hanging out' mannerisms – that form the symbology of contemporary teen coolness. This semiotic 'anatomy' is based on the interviews, observations, and studies I conducted on teens over a ten year period.

## Facial Appearance and Expression

Many of the signs that a child has become a teenager literally can be seen on his or her face. The grimaces, exaggerated contortions of the mouth to convey disgust, the coy looks projected towards a member of the opposite sex, and so on, are the facial signs that mark the onset of teenagerhood. These are acquired in large part through signifying osmosis: that is, they are biologically based behaviours whose specific formations result from peer interactions.

The study of facial signals by semioticians, psychologists, and ethologists has a rich research tradition (see, for example, Vine 1970; Wallbott 1979; Ekman 1982). The use of the face (consciously and unconsciously) to convey affective states is a phenomenon that cuts across many species. As Desmond Morris (1990: 163) has aptly put it, many animals can combine elements of facial expression in different ways so as to 'create a whole repertoire of faces, each corresponding to a special, complex mood.' Morris (163–73) goes on to remark that animals are predisposed by biology to use the ears, the eyes, and the mouth to convey their inner states. Ears, for example, can prick up when an animal is alert (dogs), twitch when it is conflicted or agitated (caracal lynxes), and flatten when it is being protective (felines). An animal's eyes can be fixed in a stare during an alert mode or in a frown during a protective mode. Mouths can be tightened, made to gape, or made to pout in order to convey, respectively, states of hostility, aggression, and amicability.

An interesting kind of facial expression documented by animal ethologists is the so-called flehmen mouth. This is a peculiar kind of facial expression, shown by many mammals, that follows intense sniffing, especially of a sexual nature. Morris (1990: 169) describes it as follows: 'The head is tilted up as the neck stretches forward. The top lip is curled upwards, exposing the upper teeth and sometimes even the upper gums. The mouth is slightly open and the animal appears to be momentarily lost in a kind of reverie, almost a trance. The impression given is that the animal is inhaling deeply and savouring the fragrance in the air.'

The concept of flehmen mouth, or lip curl, can be applied by analogical extension to describe the kind of 'mopey' expressions that are noticeable on the faces of many teens. The raising of the upper lip and the frequent dangling of the mouth are, in fact, common facial features that male teens in particular display, making them appear to be in a daze. There is a strong possibility that young males of all primate species are predisposed to display this kind of facial expression in response to sexual stimuli or thoughts. As a matter of fact, I noticed this expression frequently among the members of a teen male clique – whose verbal duelling antics I will describe in the next chapter – whenever the topic of their conversation turned to matters of sex. This facial expression ranges from a 'refined' lip curl deployed by a cool male to one of 'dopiness' displayed by so-called losers. Elvis Presley employed this form of mouth when speaking and singing, and it became a model of facial expression that many male teens of the fifties wanted to imitate.

During my field work, I never noticed flehmen mouth in the facial repertoires displayed by female teens. This came as no surprise because facial language, like any language, is gender coded. But I was able to detect several gender-coded differences consistent with those reported by the literature (e.g., Glass 1992: 48–9). They include the following:

| Male Teens | Female Teens |
|---|---|
| They tend to avoid eye contact. | They are much more likely to make eye contact |
| They tend to cock their head to the side and look at their interlocutors from an angle. | They tend to look directly at the other person. |
| They tend to stare more. | They stare much less. |
| They tend to smile less, and grin more. | They tend to smile more often, especially in the presence of males. |
| They are more inclined to 'make faces' for comical effect. | They are more likely to keep their facial expressions composed. |

Such contrasts result in large part from the osmotic acquisition of gender-coded models of behaviour in peer contexts. Needless to say, facial modelling can also have a mimetic etiology. In fact, mimesis explains the tendency of certain teens to model their facial appearances after subculture heroes (e.g., Elvis Presley, Madonna, etc.).

The face is a powerful signifier. As Jackson (1992: 44–7) has pointed out, the research has shown rather conclusively that judgments about social desirability are made first on the basis of facial appearance. No wonder, then, that both male and female teens spend so much time preparing their faces for presentation to peers. Of primary importance to facial presentation is hairstyle, which is meant to enhance the attractiveness of the face. Most teens model their hairstyles after media prototypes (mimesis) or in accordance with clique-specific grooming codes (osmosis). The latter are themselves generally derived from some external model: for example, hard rockers wear their hair long after the hairstyles of hard rock or heavy metal musicians; punkers often shave their heads, as do many of their rock heroes, and so on.

Actually, the decoration of the face, literally its 'making up' for presentation, is as old as humanity itself. Anthropologists and archaeologists have established that the cosmetic 'make-up' we use today has a long and unbroken connection with early, ritualistic fertility behaviours. It has, in other words, a basis in sexuality: the colours and designs we use to construct facial texts are sexual signifiers. Red lipstick, for instance, appears to connote the redness associated with female genitalia; men's mustaches can easily be seen to connote pubic hairs; and the list could go on and on. The point is that the human face is hardly neutral semiotically. It is constantly being 'made up' to convey messages reflective of latent biological urges and tendencies.

Two terms require some elaboration here: *signifier* and *text*. The former term was coined by Ferdinand de Saussure (1916), considered to be one of the founders of modern linguistics and semiotics. A sign, according to Saussure, was made up of two parts: a *signifier* and a *signified*. The *signifier* is the physical part of the sign, the actual substance of which it is composed (sound-waves, alphabet characters, etc.); the *signified* is the mental concept to which the signifier refers. Any signifier can be used to refer to some particular signified. For example, the verbal signifier *tree* in English and the verbal signifier *arbre* in French both refer to essentially the same signified.

The word *text* means literally a 'putting together' (from the Latin *textus*, 'something woven together') of signifiers to produce a message, consciously or unconsciously. As Hodge and Kress (1988: 6) correctly remark, for human beings a text invariably 'has a socially ascribed unity.' A text can be either verbal or nonverbal. In order for a text to have meaning, one must know the code to which the signifiers belong. If one listens to a verbal language that one does not know, all one hears are 'disembodied signifiers' – sounds, intonations, and so on, that we intuitively know cohere into verbal texts that carry some intended meaning, but to which we have no access. The 'embodiment' of the verbal signifiers occurs only when we come to know the language code to which they belong. This applies as well to all nonverbal texts, such as clothing, bodily movements, gestures, and the like. Texts are reflexes of both individual and communal experiences. When these are understood or 'appreciated,' they take on meaning or signification. Musical performances, stage plays, conversations, dance styles, religious rites, ceremonies, and so on, are the texts that we regularly construct, as individuals or as groups, both to make meaning of the world and to make meaning within it. The *context*, as the word clearly implies, is literally the surrounding or '*con*-taining' environment in which a text is encoded and decoded.

The body is not a 'neutral' biological structure. The expressions we make with our faces, the postures we assume, the gestures we make, how close we stand to each other, and so on, are all coded as socially meaningful texts. These equip us with the capacity to negotiate social actions successfully (see also Roger Schank [1984] on this point). Body parts, fluids, and shapes, too, are perceived as signifiers with specific connotations in certain contexts.

The one facial text that cuts across all the perceptions of coolness held by teen cliques is what Goffman (1959) calls facial 'poise.' As Landau (1989: 185) remarks, this kind of text enables the individual to 'suppress and conceal the tendency to be out of face or shamefaced,' which, especially among teenagers, can be severely traumatic. Keeping one's face poised in order to exude confidence and control is of the utmost importance to teens. As discussed in the previous chapter, coolness in the mainstream teen subculture involves a constant 'posing' that is staged to convey confidence. The cool teen must literally keep his or her face poised under any circumstance.

It is interesting to note, parenthetically, that individual male and female teens respond sexually to certain kinds of faces and not to others. One explanation as to why such preferences surface at adolescence is perhaps the presence in the mind of what the psychologist John Money (1986) calls 'lovemaps'. These are mental images which determine the specific kinds of features – body, facial, and so forth – that will evoke sexual arousal and love moods (such as infatuation) in an individual. According to Money, lovemaps develop around the ages of five to eight in response to various environmental experiences and influences. At adolescence, they unconsciously generate an image of what the ideal 'sweetheart' should be like, becoming 'quite specific as to details of the physiognomy, build, race and color of the ideal lover, not to mention temperament, manners and so on' (Money 1986: 19).

Eye contact is crucial as a signifying text at adolescence. The occasion and the length of time involved in making eye contact with peers are bearers of meaning. Staring can be interpreted as a challenge; 'making eyes' at someone is normally interpreted as flirtation; making eye contact earlier or later during a verbal exchange will indicate the kind of relationship one wishes to have with the interlocutor. There is nothing especially peculiar about this kind of behaviour. Humans of all ages detect eye movements unconsciously and react to them in appropriate ways. The pupil, for instance, becomes smaller during excited states, and we unconsciously pick this up. Narrowing of the eyelids, on the other hand, communicates pensiveness. The eyebrows coming closer together communicates thoughtfulness; when they rise they convey surprise. It should be noted, however, that although there are many universal aspects to facial semiosis, there is also much cultural variation involved in presenting the face. Eye contact texts vary widely from culture to culture. For instance, southern Europeans will tend to look into each other's eyes during conversation more often than North Americans.

In sum, the ability to construct facial texts is a sure sign that teenagerhood has taken hold of the child's psychosocial development. The facial texts that teenagers typically display show that biology and culture are interactive components in psychological development. The face and the body are transformed into powerful sources of signification (meaning-making) the instant that social cognition (secondness) emerges as a dominant mental gestalt on the developmental timetable of children.

## Dress Codes

It goes without saying that clothing is also a rich source of signification. At adolescence clothes become powerful signifiers of gender, sexuality, identity, and clique values. The association between clothing and sexuality is an ancient one. As Helen Fisher (1992: 253–4) aptly observes, even in the steamy jungle of Amazonia, Yanomamo men and women wear clothes for sexual modesty. A Yanomamo woman would feel as much discomfort and anguish at removing her vaginal string belt as a North American woman would if asked to remove her underwear. Similarly, a Yanomamo man would feel just as much embarrassment if his penis accidentally fell out of its encasement as a North American male would if caught literally 'with his pants down.'

During the fifties the clothes worn by the first rock stars and by media personages such as the dancers on 'American Bandstand' became the dress models for teens. Female teens donned the 'bobby socks' worn by the female dancers on 'American Bandstand' – a clothing fashion which had actually originated in the thirties (Stern and Stern 1992: 60–1); cool male teens wore leather jackets in imitation of such subculture heroes as Elvis Presley; and so on. With the fragmentation of the teen subculture into cliques from the mid sixties onwards, a corresponding diversification of clothing styles has also taken shape within it. Since the seventies teen dress styles have become more and more eclectic, and have become coded according to the particular ideological and behavioural characteristics of individual cliques.

As a case in point, consider the punk movement that started in the mid seventies. As Berger (1984: 76) observed, punks 'dyed their hair strange colors and cut it in bizarre ways, they wore unusual clothes, used props (safety pins stuck through their nostrils, for example) to attract attention and convey their message.' Although the punk movement originated as a political statement by working-class youths in England, by the time its symbology was acquired osmotically by a larger segment of the teen subculture, the punk dress code ended up being all things to all classes. As Berger (78) goes on to remark, 'the use of the fascist insignia by English punks was not an expression of a sympathy with this political philosophy, but just the opposite – a "put on," so to speak, a means of attracting attention and provoking square middle-class people.' Ewen (1988: 253) makes a similar point: 'As punk became marketable style, it became its opposite. Initially a rejection of conformist fashions, and of the false status that they carry, its appropriation by "Punky's Underground" and other outlets of the style market transforms it into an item of competitive consumption with an inflated price.' I would add that the punk dress code was used, and continues to be used, strategically to intimidate other cliques and individual teen peers. This came out during an interview session I had a few years ago with a punk rocker who pointed out to me that dressing and wearing his hair like he did made him feel powerful. 'I walk down the corridor, man, and all the shits get outta my way' was his way of conveying this to me.

The ideas of Orin E. Klapp (1969) are important for understanding the role of dress codes in the teen subculture. Klapp identifies five different modes of dress as indicators of personal style. These are mockery, dandyism, negligence, barbarism, and puritanism. The punk dress code started out as a barbaric style. And although it retains an element of barbarism, it now also conveys images of mockery and negligence, and above all else, intimidation. Teens who become punk rockers concomitantly are more inclined to be aggressive, destructive, and offensive.

Clothing texts define clique values and modes of behaviour. During one observational period spent at a number of high schools in the Toronto area several years ago, I became capable of differentiating the various dress codes adopted by specific cliques. The main clothing features of the members of the cliques I came across during my fieldwork can be summarized as follows. (Refer to the previous chapter for an explanation of the clique names.)

- Housers typically endorsed the clothing items and hairstyles of house musicians: bell-bottom pants, large belts, short, well-groomed hairstyles for the males, long flowing hairstyles for the females.

- Both male and female rockers identified with the apparel and hairstyles that hard rock and heavy metal rock musicians wore: old, ripped jeans, leather boots, scruffy shoulder-length hair, T-shirts, leather jackets.

- Male and female Mods wore black clothes, especially black leather jackets, and dyed their hair pitch black.

- Male and female bat cavers wore black clothes in a gothic style. The females also used bizarre facial make-up profusely.

- B-Boys wore baseball caps pointing backwards, T-shirts, running shoes, and (often) shorts. The wearing of baseball caps started out as an imitation of the apparel worn by many male rap musicians who generally wore the caps with the bill out to the side or facing backwards.

What Anne Hollander (1988: 452) has to say about the symbology of clothing in general seems to apply particularly to teens: 'When people put clothes on their bodies, they are primarily engaged in making pictures of themselves to suit their own eyes, out of the completed combination of clothing and body.' There are two main trends that have occurred from the seventies onwards vis-à-vis teen dress codes. First, mainstream teens have been developing increasingly expensive clothing tastes. Designer jeans, costly running shoes, expensive T-shirts, and the like have become the norm for many affluent middle-class teens. Second, there would now seem to be a 'meta-code' in teen clothing styles: that is, a generalized model of dress in the teen subculture at large which is an extrapolation and recombination of the specifics of various single-clique fashion props and accoutrements. As I write, some of these include earrings for males, multiple earrings for girls, shaved sides of the head with designs or letters carved into the hair, torn jeans, baggy pants, jeans worn backwards, ultra-long-sleeved shirts and jackets, unlaced sneakers, and baseball caps worn backwards. This meta-code excludes such single-clique fads as noserings for both males and females, multicoloured hair and make-up for both sexes, and brassieres and other lingerie worn on the outside by females. The diversity, eclecticism, and unisex nature of the current meta-code is seen by some to reflect the diversity and pluralism of North American society at large. But in a more fundamental anthropological sense, style eclecticism constitutes a normal feature of subcultural codes. It is explained by Hebdige (1979: 102) as a manifestation of subcultural *bricolage*:

In particular, the concept of *bricolage* can be used to explain how subcultural styles are constructed. In *The Savage Mind* Lévi-Strauss shows how the magical modes utilized by primitive

peoples (superstition, sorcery, myth) can be seen as implicitly coherent, though explicitly bewildering systems of connection between things which perfectly equip their users to 'think' their
own world. These magical systems of connection have a common
feature: they are capable of infinite extension because basic elements can be used in a variety of improvised combinations to
generate new meanings within them. *Bricolage* has thus been described as a 'science of the concrete' in a recent definition which
clarifies the original anthropological meaning of the term.

Fashion is also an ideological statement. Teens who see
themselves as antisocial and iconoclastic will convey this
through their clothing selections. The hippies of the sixties
and seventies dressed to emphasize 'love' and 'freedom';
punks dress to convey 'toughness' and 'nonconformity';
and so on. Uniforms have great social and symbolic significance. Military dress connotes patriotism and communal
values. However, the wearing of military uniforms for
fashion can be construed as a counter-culture statement, a
kind of parody of nationalistic tendencies, as a statement
of 'military toughness,' or as some other type of statement.
Clothing communicates. Like language, it can be en-
dearing, offensive, controversial, delightful, disgusting,
foolish, charming, and the list could go on and on.
Let us take the example of blue jeans as high-fashion
items, a trend that has swept the entire Western world in
the last few decades. Why has this happened? After all,
jeans, being cheap and strong, have traditionally been
identified as blue-collar work clothes. High-fashion articles, on the other hand, have always been expensive and
manufactured with fancy materials and fabrics. Moreover,
blue jeans are mass-produced items, whereas high-fashion
clothes are aimed at those with discriminating tastes. The
answer is, of course, that the cultural *meaning* of blue jeans
has changed dramatically. Blue jeans have been transformed by teens into fashion items and, therefore, reclas-
sified and perceived as such. This is why they are now

much more expensive than they used to be, much more exclusive, often personalized, and available even at chic boutiques. Jeans no longer symbolize a blue-collar work-force. Instead, they now symbolize the diffusion of fashion trends across all socio-economic classes, and a blurring of the demarcation between work and play. Social gradations are still, however, maintained by fashion details (brand of jeans, quality of fabric, etc.), but not by the item itself vis-à-vis other types of clothes.

To conclude my commentary on teen dress codes, I should point out that, like everything else in teenager-hood, they are ephemeral. Teen codes are highly unstable, ductile, and short-lived. Their transitory nature reflects, no doubt, the rapidly changing psychosocial constitution of adolescents generally. While some of the details of teen meta-codes can become fossilized and persist throughout life, many of them fluctuate and disappear rather quickly.

**Musical Preferences**

As argued throughout the first chapter, the history of teen-agerhood is embedded in the history of rock and roll. Rock was forged in the fifties as the musical voice of the emerging teen subculture. Fifties rock had a uniform style and its target audience consisted primarily of middle-class teens. The fragmentation of the teen subculture during the sixties entailed a concomitant differentiation in musical prefer-ences. Since the seventies the musical preferences of teens have become more and more coded according to the par-ticular world-view and behavioural styles of the clique. Nevertheless, in this area of semiosis there also emerges, typically, a meta-code that characterizes the preferences of the teen subculture at large.

As a case in point, consider rap music. As discussed in the first chapter, the rap movement originated among Afri-can-American teenagers living in ghettos or ghetto-like conditions as an artistic medium for self-expression and for denouncing the status quo. In the early nineties, rap became temporarily the musical meta-code, primarily because of its diffusion through rock programs on television. But, as I write, this is changing, as one would expect with ephemeral teen meta-codes. What will not change is the fact that rock music will continue to generate new styles and trends for future generations of teens.

Rock music emerged in the fifties to cater to teen desires and impulses. The music of Elvis Presley, Chuck Berry, Little Richard, and Jerry Lee Lewis was loud, raucous, sexual, and hedonistic. It grew out of body rhythms and urges and was directed towards stimulating these same rhythms and urges in its audiences. As rock became more sophisticated throughout the seventies, many teens felt that it had become stagnant and middle-aged. The thrill had gone out of it. The punk movement was, in fact, an attempt to recapture the spontaneous sexual barbarism of the early rock music. But it was a short-lived movement, as most teen movements are. The reason for this was its appropriation by media moguls and its promotion, in stylized form, to the general culture. Once such an appropriation takes place, the next generation of teens invariably rejects the meta-code in order to assert its autonomy from the previous generation.

What is *rock and roll*? As Stern and Stern (1992: 289) remark, rock and roll has always been 'a counterculture code, a nearly instantaneous means of tribal communication among those who were in the groove and outside the adult mainstream.' Given its crucial role in shaping the teen persona, it is important to dissect it semiotically. Above all else, rock and roll is rhythm and movement connected osmotically to sexual corporeality. From a primal, pagan-like form of frenzy (as in some heavy metal songs) to a subdued, romanticized form of swooning (as in the traditional love ballads), rock is tied to sexuality.

Love and sex have always been the primary themes of rock, reflecting the crystallization of sexual feelings at adolescence. The lyrics of the fifties ranged from love as infatuation – 'puppy love' à la Paul Anka – to explicit sex – 'breathless' à la Jerry Lee Lewis. In the sixties the lyrics of rock stars urged sweeping social changes. But this did not mean love and sex disappeared from rock. The lyrics of Bob Dylan, for instance, linked love and sex poetically (Duncan 1988: 190–1). Gone from mainstream rock, however, was the puppy love theme, probably once and for all, although it occasionally resurfaces in teeny-bopper music (as it did, for example, in the early music of the pop ensemble Wham in the eighties). The themes of love and sex in music have become more and more associated with hedonism, aggression, and exploitation – a phenomenon which perhaps reflects a larger social reality.

The increase in blatant carnality in rock music often goes unnoticed by teens, since they acquire their musical preferences osmotically and therefore unconsciously. An example is Michael Jackson's 1983 *Thriller* album and rock video, which sold some 22 million copies worldwide. The song 'Beat It' from that album shows a group of young males – aggressive and angry – looking for a fight. As the fight begins, Michael Jackson intervenes and bursts into the catchy and powerfully rhythmic 'Beat It.' As Key (1989: 19–20) reports, shortly after its release approximately three hundred university students were asked how many times they had listened to the song. The 51 per cent who had listened to it over fifty times were then asked if they knew what 'beat it' meant – it is, of course, a colloquial slang expression for male masturbation. Half of the aficionados simply said that they did not know the meaning of the expression; the remainder attempted to rationalize it – 'the music beat,' 'to beat up someone,' and so on. The survey was repeated several times with the same results. The theme of male masturbation simply escaped the conscious awareness of the teen listeners. The video even shows the dancers passing their right hands across their genital areas in a jerking, masturbatory motion. Incidentally, when told about the true meaning of the song, the informants invariably expressed disgust. The moral of this story is that teens rarely notice the sexuality inherent in the rock music they listen and dance to. They simply respond to it osmotically.

The fact that teens show a strong desire to learn dancing styles and fads should not come as a surprise. Dancing is common to all peoples and cultures. As such, it constitutes a signifying bodily text whose construction can range all the way from spontaneous movements in response to natural rhythms to 'high art' dancing, as in classical ballet. It can be said that the dance texts which cultures commonly create and employ for various social reasons are culture-specific transformations of bodily tendencies and needs.

It is virtually impossible to remain motionless for any protracted period of time. Indeed, when we are 'forced' to do so, our bodies react against it. Imagine being at, say, a concert hall during the performance of a lengthy slow movement of a piano sonata. After a little while, it is almost impossible to keep yourself perfectly still or not to cough or make some other kind of sound. The need for nearly constant movement during our waking hours is probably a residual tendency tied to an ancient survival mechanism – it is harder to attack moving prey! At the level of biology, therefore, bodily movements once enhanced our survivability. It is when we organized them, at some point in time, into patterned ones at the cultural level that *dance* emerged as a signifying text, re-enacting at this new level of mind and culture our basic bodily tendencies and needs. Dance *makes* meaning in ways that only humans can. It can therefore be devised as art, work, ceremony, ritual, entertainment, or a combination of any of these.

The association of rock dancing to corporeality has been eloquently highlighted by Grossberg (1992: 181) as follows: 'The body of youth in rock was always a body on display, to others and itself, as the mark of a celebration of energy and fun. They mattered because they were at the

heart of rock, and rock mattered. Rock touched, fragmented, multiplied, propelled the bodies of its fans. It created a
transitory body which was put into place against the various emotional narratives and alienating experiences of
youth's everyday lives.'

The shift from radio to television as a primary medium
for spreading musical trends occurred on 1 August 1981
when MTV – 'Music Television' – was founded as a
twenty-four-hour all-music television network on US ca-
ble television. Music video programming has now become a major source for shaping meta-code musical tastes.
MTV reflects how the teenage persona has changed since
the fifties. It transmits images of urgency, quickness, surre-
alism, and above all else, post-modern coolness. The MTV
look has become a ubiquitous one. As Stern and Stern
(1992: 345) aptly observe, MTV 'gave birth to a language
brilliantly suited for communicating not complicated
ideas but cool attitudes.' This new vernacular constitutes
'an ideal way to grab the attention of a generation of viewers with downsized attention spans.' MTV is performance
without drama or narration. It is all pose and posture. But
it is rather telling that MTV has itself fallen prey to the
'downsized attention spans' it was designed to captivate.
By early 1990, MTV had become all too familiar and
boring. Teen generations and attitudes change far too rapidly, more rapidly than ever before. Keeping the new
hordes of teen cliques entertained homogeneously has become a huge problem even for those who attempt to shape
teen attitudes.

## Smoking

Smoking takes on great importance as a social text in the
teen subculture, providing valuable insights into the relationship between a text – in this case, smoking behaviour –
and the particular mind-set of the teenagers who perform
it. In this section I will report on the findings of an observa-

tional research project I conducted a few years ago in the city of Toronto that probed the semiotics of smoking in teenagerhood (Danesi 1993). The findings are summarized here in a general way.

The structuring of smoking routines into discrete body movements and postures is determined by gender-coded perceptions of coolness. The teenager most likely to smoke is the one who desires to enhance his or her sexual attractiveness to peers. As Coleman and Hendry (1990: 79) observe, smoking is a behaviour that constitutes 'a perceived means of attaining attractiveness and sociability often specifically with respect to the opposite sex.'

To identify and document the features of the smoking text, a team of five fieldworkers was formed at the University of Toronto in 1989. For two years each researcher was assigned to a designated high school within metropolitan Toronto in order to record their observations on how the smoking text was performed. At key times during the day, times when teenagers would typically mingle outside the school building to talk and to engage in socially meaningful actions, a fieldworker would sit in his or her car, at a suitable distance from the congregation, recording the various features of the smoking scene and performance (body movements, postures, etc.). It is, of course, during such periods in the school day that teenagers group together to smoke.

A feature grid was drawn up for each fieldworker to fill out during the observation periods. The grid contained a series of categories relating to specific body movements:

- Pre-Smoking Routines:
  - the initial procedure employed to insert the cigarette into the mouth
  - the lighting-up procedure

- Hand and Arm Movements:
  - the fingers used to hold the cigarette

– the flicking procedure employed
– the arm movement used to insert the cigarette into
  the mouth between puffs

- Puffing Routines:
  – the inhaling procedures used
  – the exhaling procedures used

- Bodily Posture:
  – the positioning of the legs
  – the movement of the head

- Post-Smoking Routine:
  – the butting-out procedure used

Two grids with these same features were used – one for males and one for females. The fieldworkers were instructed to fill out each feature slot according to their observations, focusing on either one male or one female per observation period. Over the two years of the project, one hundred observation grids were filled out – fifty for males and fifty for females, and several photographs taken with the permission of the subjects. The observations of the fieldworkers were then conflated into general descriptive statements that reflected the most frequently recorded actions. A summary of the findings, accompanied by photos of two of the teens, follows.

It was found that females typically utilized a slow, deliberate movement to take the cigarette out of its package and to insert it into their mouths; males, on the other hand, tended to employ more abrupt, quick movements, both to take the cigarette out of its package and to insert it into their mouths. The females used the thumb and the middle finger to remove the cigarette from its package, but changed to the index and middle fingers to insert it into the mouth in a slow, flowing motion. Males, on the other hand, used the thumb and middle finger both to take out

Figure 1 - Male teen inserting cigarette into the mouth

the cigarette and to insert it into the mouth in a brusque, snappy movement (see figure 1). The only difference between females and males in lighting up the cigarette was in the rate of movement: the females tended to strike a match, and to bring the flame towards the cigarette, in a leisurely, drawn-out way, whereas males performed these same procedures with terse movements.

Females typically held the cigarette between the index and middle finger, guiding the cigarette to the lips in a languid, swooping, quasi-circular arm movement. The cigarette was normally inserted into the middle of the mouth. When the cigarette was held between the fingers, females also typically flicked the ashes with the index finger, while holding the cigarette between the thumb and middle fingers. When not flicking, the females dangled the hand holding the cigarette down by the side of the body.

Females with long hair also typically shook their hair self-consciously, allowing the hair to enshroud their faces and forcing them to pull it back away from the front of their face with a petting motion of the hand. Males, in contrast, held the cigarette between the thumb and middle finger, guiding it to the lips in a sharp, direct (short-arc) movement, often inserting the cigarette into the side of the mouth (the left or right in an asymmetrical fashion to the individual's handedness). Males either flicked their ashes in a way that was similar to the female flicking procedure (with the cigarette held between the thumb and middle finger while the index finger flicked the ashes), or, more typically, by shaking their hand to force the excess ashes to fall down to the ground.

Females normally took a longer time to inhale, drawing in air through the nostrils slowly and gradually, then holding the smoke inside the mouth for a relatively protracted period (rarely inhaling it down into the lungs), and finally exhaling it in an upward direction with the head tilted slightly back, often swinging or holding their hair back (see figure 2). Males, on the other hand, tended to inhale abruptly, holding the smoke in the mouth for a relatively short period (inhaling it down into the lungs more often than the females), and exhaling it in a downward direction (with the head slightly bent).

As for body posture, the females typically kept one leg back and one slightly ahead, with the greater portion of their weight being placed on the back leg. The head remained angled slightly to the side and looking upward with a frequent jerking motion of the hair so that it could be made to sway just before the insertion of the cigarette into the mouth. Males, on the other hand, kept both legs slightly apart – comparable to a 'horseback' or 'piggyback' posture. They kept their heads taut and looked straight ahead during puffing motions.

Finally, it was found that females typically dropped the cigarette butt and stamped it out with a foot. Males, on the

Figure 2 - Female teen exhaling

other hand, placed the butt on the thumb and hurled it away from them with the middle finger. They rarely stamped out the cigarette with their feet.

Some variation from these general schemas was recorded. However, it was not of a significant type. The picture that emerges from the above portrayals is that cigarette smoking in teenagerhood constitutes a gender-coded social text whose underlying rationale is a display of coolness. Smoking performances are coherent, regular, predictable, and anchored in socially meaningful contexts (peer interaction). In fact, it is in such peer contexts that the gender-coded smoking text is assimilated by signifying osmosis. And, indeed, when asked why they smoke, teenagers typically give answers such as, 'Because the rest of my crowd smokes,' 'It makes me look big,' 'To feel sophisticated,' and so on (Rice 1990: 304). As Rice (305) aptly puts it, smoking is a 'social coping mechanism.'

Above all else, the smoking text is a means by which perceptions of masculinity and femininity are conveyed through bodily osmosis. The slow, circular movements of the arm in females are osmotic enactments of bodily schemas that our culture perceives as 'feminine,' while the abrupt movements used by the male teenagers are osmotic performances of bodily schemas perceived as 'masculine'. These schemas are, of course, reinforced by media images.

The female's bodily schemas are, in a nutshell, osmotic displays of feminine sexuality (sensuality, voluptuousness, sultriness, etc.); the male's bodily schemas are osmotic reflexes of masculine sexuality (toughness, roughness, coarseness, etc.). When the smoking text is performed at typical gatherings of teenage cliques, it can be said to constitute a kind of unconscious mating ritual that unfolds through bodily schemas that reflect culturally coded perceptions of masculinity and femininity. This is the *subtext* underlying the visible smoking text. During such performances, the cigarette seems to take on a fetishistic quality, with rather obvious phallic connotations (see Sebeok 1989 for a semiotic analysis of fetishism). It becomes a sexual/erotic signifier that is manipulated unconsciously in paradigmatically complementary ways according to the sex of the teenager.

As Chassin, Roosmalen, and McDaniel (1992: 98) remark, the 'social dynamics of the peer environment is a crucial factor in both male and female adolescent smoking initiation and subsequent smoking behaviour.' The smoking text provides teenagers with a concrete performance routine for conforming to peer expectations of masculine or feminine coolness. Virtually all psychosocial studies of teen smoking in the last ten years have found, in fact, that the onset of smoking among teenagers is due primarily to its social value as a peer-sanctioned activity.[1] These studies

---

1   For example, Baric, MacArthur, and Fischer 1976; Green 1979; Aitken 1980; Perry et al. 1980; Flay et al. 1982; Krosnick and Judd 1982; Kniskern et al. 1983; Friedman, Lichtenstein, and Biglan 1985;

typically report that the teen smoker is perceived as having characteristics which are deemed to be social assets. These include 'popularity, disobedience, acting big, and liking to be with a group' (Chassin, Roosmalen, and McDaniel 1992: 87).

## Hanging-Out

Like the smoking text, *hanging-out* is a sexually based performance text not unlike the courtship displays observable in many other species. As Morris (1990: 185–93) has remarked, there are many kinds of specific displays – leaping, dancing, twisting, turning, and so on – that animals perform to initiate breeding relations. Hanging-out is a display of this kind that typically can be observed in teen congregations. It inheres in a controlled form of bodily movement configured by intense slackness, sluggishness, and lethargy. Indeed, the term 'hanging-out' is an appropriate way to describe how the arms are left to hang or dangle on the sides of the body, how all body movements are slackened, and how teens convey total nonchalance, indifference, and insouciance.

In hanging-out situations, the males occasionally try to look 'tough,' through aggressive posturing, when other male peers or rivals approach the congregation. The toughness posture is put on to reinforce perceptions of masculinity. Its symbology involves menacing facial expressions and vulgar language. This kind of posturing, however, is not as dangerous as it might seem at first. As Morris (1990: 193) puts it, courtship displays in many species may look menacing or comical to outsiders, 'but to the species concerned they are a crucial communication device at a key stage in the reproductive cycle.'

The symbology of hanging-out is, of course, acquired through signifying osmosis. The bodily features that

Pederson and Lefcoe 1985; Skinner et al. 1985; Kannas 1985; Reek and Drop 1987; Chassin, Roosmalen, and McDaniel 1992).

hanging-out entails are picked up in contexts such as the school yard and the shopping mall. During such gatherings teens invariably put on hanging-out performances. The modern shopping mall provides a particularly appropriate setting for hanging-out displays, because it contains the stage props (food outlets, smoking areas, etc.) and provides characters (other teens, adult spectators, etc.) that give emphasis and social meaning to them. In a certain sense, the mall is similar to what ethologists call a *lek* (Immelmann and Beer 1989: 174): '[A lek is] a communal mating area within which males hold small territories, which they use solely for courtship and copulation. Females are attracted to a lek by the displays of the males and then choose mating partners from among them, usually favoring males with territories in the center.'

Actually, the shopping mall has become a popular *hangout* not only for teens, but for virtually everyone living in an urban or suburban setting. It is hardly just a locus for shopping. The mall satisfies several symbolic needs at once: it provides a space for human socialization and thus alleviates loneliness and boredom; it provides a theatrical atmosphere proclaiming the virtues of a consumeristic utopia; it imparts a feeling of security and protection; it protects against the world of cars, mechanical noises, and exhaust pollution; it provides protection from the elements; and it conveys a feeling of control and organization. The mall is placeless and timeless – there is no sense of aging or of time passing in its ambience. No wonder then that teens feel at home in these self-contained cities, these veritable 'fantasylands' where teens literally can leave their school and family problems 'outside.'

# 4
# Pubilect: The Language of Teenagerhood

*Ever since the Middle Ages, when young men left the supervision of their families and flocked to such centers of learning as Paris and Bologna to pursue learning and life in a community of scholars, students have created an ever-changing set of words and phrases to strengthen their group identity and to set themselves off from others.*
Eble (1989: 11)

On 15 March 1987, the *Washington Post* published an article that, in a rather eloquent fashion, claimed that slang reflected the teenager's overall temperament. The following passage from the article is cited here because it makes the important point that teenage language reflects subcultural solidarity and aids in the formation of a mindset:

There was a time when we spoke in code: the language of adolescence. Adults still cling tenaciously to the vocabulary that they grew up on, those words that were once essential to both communicating and establishing a mindset. But, in the halls of schools across the land, wild-eyed youths are flinging freshly invented words and newly coined phrases at one another with the hope of including a Few and, at the same time, excluding Us.

Young people have, in fact, resorted to slang words since the Middle Ages in order to strengthen peer-group identity and to set themselves apart from adults. For instance, medieval university students coined the word *lupi*, 'wolves,' to refer to spies who reported someone for using the vernacular instead of Latin. If slang has a specific social function, then it can hardly be considered a form of aberrant communicative behaviour. In fact, it is the verbal equivalent of the smoking text described in the previous chapter. It is part of a meta-code that adolescents acquire through signifying osmosis.

So, in this chapter I will start off by distinguishing between slang and the teen verbal meta-code (Danesi 1988, 1989a). I will then describe the specific features of this meta-code and the kinds of discourse strategies it encompasses. After that, I will illustrate how it takes on specific clique features by describing the verbal duelling antics of a typical all-male teen clique (between stages one and two of Dunphy's cliquing cycle as described in the second chapter). I will conclude by reporting briefly on data that I have recently collected on Italian teens which can be used as a template for making cross-cultural comparisons.

The peculiar intonations, words, and other modes of speech that teens pick up from each other reveal how they come to interpret themselves, others, and their environment. Knowing what teenagers talk about, and why they talk the way that they do, has obvious implications for parents and educators alike.

## Pubilect vs. Slang

The research on the language of teenagers has made it clear to me that teenage discourse is hardly reducible to slang status.[1] On the contrary, the studies show that the ways in which teenagers speak constitutes a distinct and

1  For example, Gusdorf 1965; Britton 1970; Rector 1975; Adelman 1976; Leona 1978; Labov 1972, 1982; Romaine 1984; Rizzi 1985; Shapiro 1985; Eckett 1988; Nippold 1988; Danesi 1988, 1989, 1993;

easily recognizable discourse code that children approaching puberty acquire unconsciously from their teen peers. Teen speech is, in other words, socially coded behaviour that derives its characteristic features from signifying osmosis. Teens pick up their ways of speaking in adherence and conformity to peer-shaped models of verbal behaviour.

Notwithstanding this conspicuous property of teen talk, most researchers continue to refer to it as slang. But, in my view, it is to be considered more of a social dialect, one which I prefer to call *pubilect*. Pubilect can, therefore, be defined simply as the social dialect of puberty. It is a meta-code in the same sense that mainstream dress and musical styles are meta-codes. Moreover, like all codes it demonstrates cross-clique variation.

Hudson (1984: 46–7), too, sees a difference between slang in general and what he calls, more specifically, *teenage slang*. The latter is the code 'used by teenagers to signal the important difference they see between themselves and older people' (46). Indeed, adults frequently resort to slang to colour or emphasize their messages (Hughes 1991). But for teens, pubilect is their primary verbal means of communication with peers. So, it can be said that slang is a speech option available to the population at large; pubilect, on the other hand, is the particular code used by teens to speak among themselves.

Predictably, pubilect is an oral and ephemeral code, continually adapting to the ever-changing requirements of peer socialization and clique evolutionary tendencies. The data I have reported on elsewhere (Danesi 1988, 1989a, 1993b) show it has a restricted discourse range. Teens will talk mainly about what is of direct interest to their clique members. If the universe of potential discourses is subdivided into three main thematic areas – talking about ab-

De Paoli 1988; Eble 1989; Munro 1989; Andersson & Trudgill 1990; Eder 1990; Slossberg-Anderson 1990; Cameron 1992; Labov 1992.

stractions (ideas, concepts, etc.), talking about things and events, and talking about others – then it has become obvious to me that teens spend most of their time talking about others in their immediate environment (friends, clique members, family members, etc.). This is, of course, typical of a secondness form of cognition. Even when teens talk about such abstractions or events as alcohol consumption, music, party-related activities, and sex, they do so in reference specifically to others ('I hate that music, 'cause Barb likes it'; 'Makin' out is great, especially with Marge'; etc.). In a nutshell, the domain of teenage discourse is centred around the immediacy of present events and the people who populate their immediate world.

At this point it is perhaps useful to return to the concept of *signifying osmosis* as proposed in this book. It can now be said that a code like pubilect is the result of signifying *bilateral* osmosis. The osmotic acquisition of behavioural traits from peer contact is obviously a *bilateral* process: that is, peers influence each other. Whereas *unilateral* osmosis involves any organism in isolation as the receiver and processor of physiologically detectable signals in the immediate environment (Meyer-Eppler 1959), *bilateral* osmosis involves the reception and processing of signals by participating organisms in the surrounding environment. The systematic interaction and pattern of responses in which these organisms participate defines the communication system for the species to which they belong. The common factor in all biological organisms is the fact that bilateral osmosis allows for the instantaneous reception and interpretation of signals present in the immediate environment. As Ruesch (1972: 83) has appropriately pointed out, bilateral osmotic communication is the 'organizing principle of nature.'

**Features**

What is pubilect like? It has several traits that make it immediately recognizable. A few years ago, I was able to record on tape spontaneous speech samples of adolescents talking to each other in context at school and at parties. The recordings were made casually without the awareness of the teenagers, so as to avoid intrusion into their verbal behaviour (Danesi 1989a). Other teenagers with hidden tape recorders agreed to gather appropriate speech samples for me, and the data that I was able collect led me to postulate the presence of three basic discourse programming categories: *Emotive Language Programming, Connotative Language Programming,* and *Clique-Coded Language Programming.*

*Emotive Language Programming*

Above all else, pubilect, in all its varieties, is an emotive code. It shows, for instance, a tendency towards exaggeration, especially in tone and voice modulation. This bears witness, no doubt, to the need of teenagers to project their subjective awareness of feelings. When teenagers say things like 'Amazing!,' 'Yuch!,' and 'Far out!' with prolonged stress, accompanying gesticulations, facial contortions, and so on, they are drawing attention to their feelings and attitudes. Hesitation mannerisms, such as the constant use of 'like' throughout their sentences, indicate that they have, in fact, a hard time relating factual experiences. In social interactions, teenagers tend to think emotionally, not logically. Emotive Language Programming (ELP) refers to this feature of pubilect: that is, ELP refers to the common tendency among teens to speak with strategic devices and intensified language markers (increased or decreased rates of speech delivery, overwrought intonation contours, expressive voice modulations, etc.).

Utterances such as 'He's sooooo cute!,' 'She's faaaaar out!,' and 'That's amaaaazing!' exemplify the common ELP pattern of overstressing highly emotional words by prolonging their tonic vowels. Utterances such as 'We call-

ed her up (?)' (intonation contour like a question) – 'but
she wasn't there (?)' (same contour) – 'so we hung up (?)'
(same contour) show regular rising contours (as in so-
called tag questions). This typical ELP discourse trait
probably indicates the need to ensure the full participation
of the interlocutor in the teen's mind-world. ELP also
manifests itself in the abundant use of interjec-tions,
exclamations, and grunts ('Yuch!,' 'Yeah!,' 'Holy,!' 'What's
happening?,' etc.), which reflect the adolescent's need to
draw continual attention to his or her feelings, opinions, or
attitudes. Swear words, too, are manifesta-tions of ELP.
Exaggerated irony or facetiousness ('Get off my case!'),
and the use of what Andersson and Trudgill (1990: 18–19)
call fillers, such as the word 'like' ('Like, I called him up,
but, like, he wasn't sure, if he, like, could come '), reflecting
an unconscious hesitancy in expression, are other features
of ELP. Words and expressions such as 'awesome,' 'major,'
'this sucks,' 'I'm pissed off,' 'what a shithead,' and all
kinds of vulgarisms (especially the word 'fuck') reveal a
constant and persistent need to convey emotion, to make
sure that one's feelings come out forcibly in the discourse
text.

To linguists there is nothing particularly surprising
about this feature of pubilect. Phylogenetically, speech
must have functioned as an audio-oral modelling system
at some early point in evolution. Residual examples of this
func-tion continue to abound. We often use alliteration, or
the repetition of sounds, for various effects: for example,
'sing-song,' or 'no-no.' We commonly lengthen sounds for
emphasis, as in 'Yesssss!' or 'Noooooo!' We regularly use
intonation to express emotional states, to emphasize or to
shock: 'Are you absolutely sure?,' 'Noooooo way!' The language of cartoons and comic books, incidentally, is replete
with sound-modelling verbal techniques – 'Zap!,' 'Boom!,'
'Pow!' Verbal descriptions are, more often than not, sound-
imitative – a mean individual, for instance, is typically
compared to a snake and described as being 'slithery,'

'slippery,' or 'sneaky.' The list could go on and on. ELP is above all else a sound-based form of meaning-making. Although the language that a group or culture speaks develops into a primarily symbolic code over time, there is plenty of evidence – both in how the child learns to speak and in the nature of words themselves – that it was forged originally as a sound-modelling code. In his great 1939 novel *Finnegans Wake*, James Joyce makes the sound of words reverberate in our minds, stimulating in us memories of how they must have literally 'sounded' to us when we first learned to speak. The power of Joyce's prose lies in its ability to penetrate the deepest layers of verbal sound-making, and to put up to the light of consciousness our hidden exiences – the first fears, the first pleasures, and so on, that it allowed us to encode. A single word in Joyce's narrative evokes a series of other words, which are related to the first via sound or rhythm patterns. Words are stored by the mind not in terms of semantic fields or alphabetic categories, but in terms of what might be called 'experiential contiguity': words are related mnemonically to each other via sound and rhythm so that a particular sound or rhythmic pattern in one word evokes that same sound or pattern in another. This is why Joyce coins words throughout his novel on the basis of their resemblances to the sounds and rhythms of other words, thus evoking the primordial creative force of language. And this is why Joyce's syntax is not based on conceptual categories, but experiential ones. His 'storyline' can only be 'experienced,' not 'understood.'

The term *emotive* was also used by Roman Jakobson (1960) to refer to the fact that a speaker's emotions, attitudes, social status, and so on, converge to shape the specific ways in which he or she will construct a verbal text in a particular context. The emotive function varies in degree according to the type of message: poetic texts, for example, tend to be more emotive than information-transfer texts. Jakobson calls the effect – physical, psychological, social, and so forth – that the verbal text has on the receiver as the *conative* function.

The ELP category was found on the spontaneous con-versation tapes as well as on tapes of interviews I con-ducted with several teens (Danesi 1989a), suggesting that ELP is a dominant category in the teen's programming of discourse. By counting all the distinct sentences (complete and elliptical) uttered by the subjects, and by expressing those sentences deemed to be manifestations of the ELP category as a percentage of the total, I found that ELP occurs roughly 65 per cent of the time in adolescent discourse.

ELP is also gender coded. For instance, male teens con-sistently use more hesitation devices and fillers (Anders-son and Trudgill 1990: 18); female teens, on the other hand, are more likely to use 'tag' endings such as 'ya' know?' Cool males and females, however, share many of the same ELP features: a slow and deliberate mode of delivery, an abundant use of swear words, and a propensity to domi-nate a communicative interaction, treating the interlocu-tors as if they were mere spectators.

*Connotative Language Programming*

A second characteristic feature of pubilect is its tendency to be highly connotative. The coining of new words – 'twit,' 'bubble-head,' 'slime-bucket,' and so on – to de-scribe the people and events in their immediate social con-text is at the core of teens' symbological organization of reality. Connotative Language Programming (CLP) refers to the tendency of teenagers to coin descriptive words or to extend their meaning in highly connotative ways. Con-notation is at the core of the adolescent's verbal modelling of reality.

Much of CLP is based on metaphor. In the last two de-cades the plethora of research on metaphor in cognitive psychology and linguistics has made it impossible to assign it to some subcategory vis-à-vis other semantic systems of language. In 1977, Howard Pollio and his associates showed that the average English-speaker invents in the order of three thousand metaphors per week (Pollio et al. 1977). Work such as this has clearly shown that metaphor is not simply a discourse ornament or option. Rather, it constitutes a fundamental aspect of discourse programming.

Although interest in metaphor is as old as Aristotle, the experimental study of its relation to cognition and communication is a relatively recent phenomenon. Since the seventies, attention to metaphor on the part of scientists from diverse fields has become so intense that it is virtually impossible to skim even the surface of the data their research has generated. As Hoffman (1983: 35) put it a decade ago, metaphor has become 'a very hot topic' in the sciences and in philosophy. What stands out most from this research is that metaphor is an intrinsic feature of language and cognition (see Danesi 1989b, Nuessel 1991, for summaries of the relevant findings and theories).

Research on metaphor has revealed many intriguing things about discourse programming in general. It has shown, for instance, that literal paraphrases never quite encompass the metaphorical message, that a large area of conceptualization is embedded in metaphor, that children produce metaphors regularly in order to express physical resemblances between objects, that huge chunks of discourse are based on metaphorically structured concepts, and so on. The catalogue of findings on metaphor has become an extensive one indeed. Suffice it to say that, when considered cumulatively, the research seems to suggest that at least a portion of the human mind is 'programmed' to think metaphorically.

The work of Lakoff and Johnson in linguistics (e.g., Lakoff and Johnson 1980; Lakoff 1987; Johnson 1987) is perhaps the most germane to the discussion of CLP. The essential claim made by these two scholars is that our most common concepts are forged via metaphor. According to Lakoff and Johnson, metaphor probably underlies the representation of most of our common concepts, and it structures, indeed guides, the ways in which we perceive, think, and act.

CLP can be described in terms of metaphorical discourse programming as follows: it is a largely unconscious strategy that translates into words the teenager's perceptions of others. As an example of how it might work, consider the following hypothetical situation. Let us say that a female teen dislikes some male teen in her grade nine class. She dislikes him because he is not 'cool.' He is, instead, labelled a 'nerd' or 'loser' by her friends. His advances repulse her. Seeing him as a tall, gangly, and pimply individual, she might refer to him as something like a 'pimple-pole.' In having invented this metaphor, the female teen has taken several aspects of the male teen's physical appearance – facial appearance (pimples), lankiness and height (pole) – and forged them into an appropriate descriptive term that reveals how she feels. This is essentially how CLP works.

In an intriguing study, Andersson and Trudgill (1990: 88–9) asked fifty-five teenagers aged thirteen to fourteen to give expressions for a 'stupid person.' Their aim was, clearly, to examine the workings of what I have called the CLP feature of pubilect. Among the words produced by the adolescents are the following self-explanatory metaphors: *'wally, dingo, dozy, dodo, drip, dickhead, goof, thicko, nerd, banana, peabrain, knob, spasmo, dildo, burgerbrain, dappo.'*

Perhaps the most revealing finding vis-à-vis the CLP category came from an interview session I conducted several years ago. Three thirteen-year-olds were asked to explain, in their own way, the semantic differences between 'nerd,' 'dork,' and 'geek.' One informant defined a 'nerd' as 'a social outcast ... male, greasy, studies chemistry all night long ... someone I would never talk to.' Another described a 'dork' as: 'more socially acceptable, although he always bumps into people and drops things.' The third informant added: 'Dorkness is not a permanent state.' One of the informants then defined a 'geek' as 'someone who doesn't take showers, who is slimy, greasy, and drippy.' Another pointed out that there was a particular kind of 'geek,' known specifically as a 'leem' in her school, who was to be viewed as particularly odious. He was someone 'who just wastes oxygen.'

I was also able, during the 1991–2 school year, to collect data on how metaphor underlies the ways in which teenage girls attending a school in downtown Toronto talked about the boys in their school. With the help of a student, the following metaphorical expressions were compiled. In all cases the metaphorical expression used can be translated simply as 'he's handsome':

| Metaphorical concept | Examples |
| --- | --- |
| Ironic imitations of the 'negative effect' the male teen is perceived to make on girls | 'He's nasty.' 'He's bad.' 'He's down.' 'He's heavy.' 'He's dope.' |
| Comparisons of the male teen to animals and associated concepts | 'He's a stag.' 'He's a fly.' 'He's wild.' 'He's a catch.' |
| Comparison of the male teen to rare and admirable objects, entities, or places | 'He's a Ferrari.' 'He's Park Avenue.' 'He's divine.' 'He's a god.' 'He's an Adonis."' 'He's a diamond.' |
| Perceptions of the male | 'He's hot.' |

| teen in terms of sexually stimulating body states | 'He's a burning hunk of love.'<br>'He sizzles.'<br>'He's so cool.' |
|---|---|
| Perceptions of the male teen as an edible food (implying a desire to 'eat him' sexually) | 'He's full of beef.'<br>'He's a stud muffin.'<br>'He's a burger.'<br>'He's sweet.'<br>'He's got great buns.' |
| Portrayals of the male teen in terms of visual, particularly sculpted, works of art (thus imbuing him with an aesthetic quality) | 'He's a work of art.'<br>'He's chiselled.'<br>'He's a fine piece.'<br>'He's a centrefold.'<br>'He's picture perfect.'<br>'He's an 8 by 10.' |

A recent study by Cameron (1992) shows that a similar kind of metaphorically based CLP underlies the terms used by male adolescents to refer to the penis. Cameron found that, in addition to the usual 'dick,' 'prick,' 'cock,' 'dong,' and 'shaft' terms prevalent in the culture at large, the informants also referred to the penis as a person ('willie,' 'his excellency,' 'the Hulk,' etc.), an animal ('snake,' 'cobra,' 'eel,' etc.), a tool ('screwdriver,' 'drill,' 'jackhammer,' 'chisel,' etc.), a weapon ('squirt gun,' 'love pistol,' 'passion rifle,' 'pink torpedo,' etc.), and a foodstuff ('love popsicle,' 'wienie,' 'pork,' etc.).

Eble (1989) has provided an extensive survey of the semantic 'dynamics' involved in the formation of teen words. Her examples are a few years old and were collected from first-year college students (late adolescents). Nevertheless, glossaries such as hers (see also Munro 1989; Burke 1991, 1992) are cases in point of how pervasive and systematic the CLP category is. The dynamics of CLP include the following:

| Dynamics | Examples |
|---|---|
| Recycling of old words | 'preesh' (from appreciate) |
| Affixation | 'megabitch'<br>'geekdom'<br>'pizzafest' |
| Word combining | 'party animal'<br>'pizza dude' (one who delivers pizza)<br>'beam out' (daydream)<br>'check out' (look at, observe)<br>'jell out' (relax, do nothing) |
| Piecing together parts of words | 'vomatose' (disgusting = vomit + comatose) |
| Shortening words and phrases | 'bod' (body)<br>'bro' (brother)<br>'spaz' (spastic) |
| Acronymy | 'BK' (Burger King)<br>'MLA' = massive lip action (passionate kissing) |
| Onomatopoeia | 'barf' (vomit)<br>'yuck' (disgust)<br>'blimp boat' (obese person) |
| Rhyming | 'balls to the walls' (tense, frantic situation)<br>'sight delight' (good-looking male) |

| | |
|---|---|
| Rapping (borrowed from African-American discourse) | 'Yo' (greeting expression)<br>'blow' (sing)<br>'jive' (to misinform) |
| Changing the meaning of ordinary words | 'easy' (flexible, not difficult to please)<br>'radical' (wild at a party) |
| Metaphor and metonymy | 'horn' (telephone)<br>'cancer stick' (cigarette)<br>'dog' (unattractive person)<br>'wimp dog' (male with little personality) |

In general, CLP is a means by which teens can make value judgments about others without commitment. As Eble (1989: 93) puts it: 'Slang [pubilect] provides [teens] with automatic affirmative and negative verbal responses for typical situations with peers, allowing the users to appear to make value judgments without actually taking a stand or exposing their feelings. Slang [CLP] provides the words to soothe, commiserate, and encourage in bad times, and to affirm, approve, and tease in good times.'

The data collected by Teresa Labov (1992) reveal some interesting aspects of CLP that are germane to the discussion here. She was able to quantify in percentages the degree to which college students (late adolescents) recognized various CLP terms. For instance, the term 'jock' was recognized by 90.42 per cent of her informants, whereas 'fleabag' produced only a 6.51 per cent recognition rate. This indicates rather conspicuously that there is much regional variation in pubilect, and that only some of the words coined by teens gain general currency or meta-code status. In addition to 'jock,' Labov (348) reports the following words as having achieved a wide diffusion: 'suck' (96.17 per cent), 'cool' (91.57 per cent), 'wasted' (88.89 per cent), and 'awesome' (84.67 per cent). She also provides variation data for the definitions given to various terms, as well as for the terms more likely to be known by males vs. females, whites vs. African-Americans, city vs. suburban dwellers, public vs. private school students, East vs. West Coast informants, and first- vs. second-year college students. The picture that emerges from her study shows two general things. First, there are some expressions that cut across all varieties of pubilect (as, for example, the word 'cool'). These cohere into the pubilectal meta-code. Second, there is much diversity and variation in how teenagers speak.

## Clique-Coded Language Programming

Pubilect also varies according to the specific clique to which a teenager belongs. Clique-Coded Language Programming (CCLP) refers to the fact that pubilect constitutes a means for establishing peer-clique bonds. It also refers to the kinds of discourse that each clique engages in. Teens will talk mainly about what is of direct interest to their clique members. As Cooper and Anderson-Inman (1989: 239) aptly point out, CCLP is ensconced in strategic behaviour: 'Gaining control over marked linguistic features shows a growing competence in the use of communicative strategies that both realize and regulate behaviour and speech patterns appropriate to gender and peer group membership.'

It should be pointed out that the ELP, CLP, and CCLP categories are general properties of pubilectal codes. The tokens generated by each category are, of course, subject to a high degree of variation and ephemerality. Indeed, the very fact that the emotive and connotative specifics seem to change with extreme rapidity is proof that the categories are highly productive ones. Teen vocabularies in particular are highly unstable. As Eble (1989: 12) points out, 'by comparison with vocabulary change in the language as a whole, which sometimes takes centuries, the rate of change in slang vocabularies is greatly accelerated.' Interestingly, some words have more staying power than others: 'cool' and 'chick' (female teen) go back to the fifties; 'stoned' (inebriated, drugged out) comes out of the sixties; 'wheels' (car), and 'bummer' (unpleasant experience) have been around since the seventies.

## Situational Focusing

Pubilect is highly dependent on the strategic and tactical value of the words and intonation modalities chosen by the speakers. Communication is a goal-oriented activity, and language provides the tools that speakers utilize to enact or externalize their 'ego-dynamic' states, to use Renzo Titone's (1977) term. Interlocutors are continually engaged in bringing about the realization of self-centred agendas and goals through negotiation, manipulation, suasion, and other strategies. Di Pietro (1987: 41) refers to this phenomenon as *strategic interaction*, or the purposeful and artful use of language when dealing with others.

The study of pubilect shows that ego-dynamic states are particularly operative in the programming of discourse. The teenager's affective responses to the world seem to guide the choice of words and structures he or she uses when speaking. Teens often deliberately elaborate on the literal or information content (IC) of a message in such a way as to take their listener 'into the situation' to which he or she apparently wants to draw attention. This particular kind of strategy can be called 'situational focusing' (SF). The following is an example of an SF-structured utterance. Note that in the SF message the teen has portrayed his or her job scene and feelings about it rather graphically.

| IC-Structured Utterance | SF-Structured Utterance |
|---|---|
| A teen might wish to relay a message with the following IC structure to one of | The same teen, having become tired of his or her job, might wish to relay |

his or her peers: 'I've been working at McDonald's.'

this same message as follows: 'I've been shovelling burger patties for a year.' (This is different from the IC-structured one primarily in its portrayal of the work scene.)

The study of discourse and human interaction boasts a long and illustrious tradition.[2] The pivotal research of such scholars has shown that discourse goes well beyond grammatically constrained information transfers. It involves determining *who* says *what* to *whom*, *where* and *when* it is said, and *how* and *why* it is said. In other words, it involves contextual parameters such as the setting, message contents, participants, and goals of each interlocutor. All these contextual factors are critical in determining the specific form a speech act will assume (a good recent review of the work on speech as a transactional process can be found in Goodwin and Duranti 1992).

Situational Focusing can be defined as an interactive strategy deployed by a teen speaker to relay his or her feelings to a peer by bringing the peer verbally into the realm of the speaker's life experiences. It is different from conative effect, Jakobson's (1960) widely used term for any speech act aiming to have some effect on the listener. It is, however, quite similar to what Goodwin and Goodwin (1992: 181) have recently labelled 'assessments': namely, strategies which 'provide participants with resources for displaying evaluations of events and people in ways that are relevant to larger projects that they are engaged in.'

How does SF work? Like a lens scanning the emotionally meaningful areas in one's life domain, the SF-structured

2  For example, Wittgenstein 1922; Malinowski 1923; Bühler 1934; Firth 1951; Austin 1962; Joos 1967; Searle 1969, 1976; Hymes 1972; Halliday 1975, 1985; Goffman 1978; Tannen 1990.

utterance spotlights specific features in this domain for the interlocutor to notice. In this fashion, the speaker is able to provide a commentary either on his or her affective state or perception of a situation. In a way, SF attests to the veracity of the Italian proverb *la lingua batte dove il dente duole* (literally, 'the tongue touches the hurting tooth'): that is, feeling-states will out, no matter what.

In my own fieldwork with teens, I would jot down in a small notebook any utterance that I recognized or suspected to be an instance of SF. The few examples cited here, which are selections from my 'linguist's little black book,' will suffice to illustrate how SF typically manifests itself in pubilect:

| SF Token | IC Analysis |
|---|---|
| 'Yeah, I guess looking into a frying pan all day is, like, OK.' | Uttered to me by a female adolescent commenting upon her part-time job at McDonald's in an obvious attempt to make me understand how boring and mindless her job was, even though she was glad to have it. |
| 'It's been, well, a year of, uh, studying the burping capacities of the human male. | Uttered to me by a female adolescent after breaking up with her boyfriend, in order to convey to me ironically how hard it had been to get used to his idiosyncrasies. What appeared to irritate and annoy her the most was his burping behaviour. |
| 'I can't quite get my pole | Uttered by a male teen to |

cranked up to do it
any more.'

his friend to relay to him
how breaking up with his
girlfriend had decreased
his sex urge ('pole' = penis)

'Well, she's, like, fifteen
and still hanging around
the house on Saturday
nights.

Uttered to me by a teen
whose friend was not as
socially oriented as she
wanted her to be.
Obviously the teen who
spoke to me was a regular
party-goer.

## Verbal Duelling

An especially interesting aspect of discourse among teens
is its use in attaining power within the clique. Over a decade ago, Maltz and Borker (1982: 207) noticed that male
teenagers in particular achieved relative status in the fluc-
tuating hierarchy of their clique by learning how to manipulate their verbal interactions with peers. A male teen typically does this by using language, in all its communicative
modalities, to assert a position of dominance, to attract and
maintain an audience, and to assert himself when other
speakers have the floor. In effect, the Maltz and Borker
study demonstrated that teenage boys are continuously
testing the verbal skills of one another in an attempt to
gain the 'upper hand.' Those with ineffectual verbal skills
will either become outcasts or be compelled to accept low-
er status within the peer clique hierarchy.

To gather data on this aspect of teen discourse, members
of a male adolescent clique living in Toronto were recorded
in spontaneous conversational settings over a two-month
period. This clique was between stages one and two in
Dunphy's (1963) cyclical model of cliques (see chapter
two). It consisted of ten male teens between the ages of
fourteen and sixteen, of different racial and ethnic back-

grounds who attended a typical suburban high school in northwestern Toronto. All of the informants came from middle- to upper-middle-class homes. The teens perceived and labelled themselves as Norms (see chapter two), a kind of 'average' peer clique with no particular distinguishing characteristics.

The data-gathering method consisted of two procedures. The first was designed to record spontaneous oral conversation samples uttered in casual interactional settings. In order to ensure that the informants were not aware that they were being recorded, one of the teens agreed to conceal a tape recorder on him when he interacted with his friends. After several 'concealed' recording sessions the other clique members became aware they were being recorded. Nevertheless, they allowed me to continue recording them, provided I deleted all references to specific persons. As it turned out, the knowledge that they were being recorded did not seem to affect the spontaneity of their discourse. This is not atypical. As Milroy (1980: 61) also discovered, obligations to the group are so powerful that they tend to override any influence recording equipment or interviewers might have. Five hours of spontaneous conversation texts, uttered in appropriate contexts (in the school yard, at parties, at hang-outs, etc.), were recorded during the two-month period. The second procedure involved me participating temporarily in group activities. This allowed me to hang out with the group and to observe firsthand how the members interacted.

During the hanging-out sessions, it became obvious to me that the four teens contending for clique leadership did most of the speaking. The less powerful members were mainly silent or else answered when addressed. The group referred to itself simply as 'the guys.' Females were excluded from the 'intimacy' of group interactions. Nevertheless, on some occasions females were involved in the conversation, especially during party scenarios. The presence of females did not seem to alter the discourse styles of the clique members.

The ELP feature manifested itself continuously on the tapes in the form of a 'stoned out' delivery style. This description reflects the tendency of the group's leaders to prolong vowels as if mumbling or drawling, and to end with a slightly raised intonation, which gave the impression that the speaker was slightly 'wasted' or 'stoned out' on drugs or alcohol. It was remarkably similar to the drawl-like style of delivery associated with the movies made by Cheech and Chong in the seventies and eighties. The following are a few examples of this ELP feature:

What haaappened to your heeaaad bitch?

Loook at this guy's haaair maaaan!

I liiiike thiiiis maaaan, thiiiis would be a fuuuckin' ruuush maaaan!

Coool maaan!

The constant use of obscene words (another ELP feature) was deployed as a strategy both to convey solidarity and to shock outsiders. The constant use of such words, however, seems eventually to decrease their emotive effect and they become mere conversational gambits or verbal protocols. By the end of the two months, when the shock effect had subsided for me, the semantic load of the words became virtually nonexistent.

I was also able to record plenty of examples that documented the occurrence of both clique-specific and meta-code CLP features. These included:

*Clique-Specific CLP:*
- 'Sock,' 'Sock me,' 'Ya' got socked' ('to sock' means 'to punch') = an expression that is used in retort to someone having been disgraced or degraded.

- 'Cheap,' 'Don't do the cheap' = to do something that is against clique rules, by avoidance or by 'taking an easy way out.'

- 'Kooratz' = this particular clique's term for 'geek,' 'dork,' or 'loser.'

- 'He got Mansonned' (referring to Charles Manson, the convicted killer and cult leader) = someone who has been vitiated or humiliated.

*Meta-code CLP:*
- 'That guy's a looooser maaaan' = a socially undesirable peer.

- 'That chick's wild': 'chick' = attractive adolescent female/'wild' = greatly attractive

- 'I'm so hammered man I think I'm going to heave': 'hammered' = inebriated/'to heave' = to vomit.

- 'Cool maaan': 'cool' = socially desirable behaviour.

- 'He's seriously wasted maaan': 'wasted' = inebriated

It should be noted that the teens perceived CLP items to be specific to clique discourse styles and context-sensitive. Out-of-context uses, as well as uses by non-peers, invariably evoked insults from group members. This is, in fact, what happened the few times I used one of their clique-specific CLP items for conversational purposes.

The frequent use of the word 'man' requires a special mention. It occurred, in 'stoned out' style, almost as consistently as four-letter words. As a feature of CCLP it obviously functions as a term for clique identity. At the same time it is a verbal acknowledgment of the group members' gender – the primary condition for clique membership.

The strategic use of aggressive and obscene language in verbal duels plays an extremely important role in asserting leadership within male cliques. Eder (1990: 67) has labelled this form of verbal duelling *ritual conflict:* 'Ritual conflict typically involves the exchange of insults between two peers, often in the presence of other peers who serve as an audience. This activity is usually competitive in nature, in that each male tries to top the previous insult with one that is more clever, outrageous, or elaborate.'

The goal during ritual exchanges is to 'keep one's cool' by not letting the opponent realize that one is wavering. Eder (74) points out that 'the ability to respond to even personal insults in a nonserious manner is a critical skill needed for successful participation in ritual insulting.' Verbal conflict skills are developed through frequent participation in duelling exchanges. For this reason, those individuals who hang out more with the group seem to get a firmer command of the conflict techniques needed to succeed at verbal duels (Labov 1972: 258). The audience acts as a kind of critic. If the exchange ends with someone verbally destroying the other, the audience will invariably proceed to ridicule and defame the loser. The following example of audience mockery occurred after one such exchange:

Ouch! Ya' got rocked maaan!

(laughter) Ya' got burned maaan!

Verbal duels are staged for the purpose of gaining power. They allow clique members to vanquish opponents symbolically. Winning strategies invariably involve a high degree of ELP and CLP abilities that have been deployed to create effective insulting language. This kind of skill is praised highly by the group. The following ironic retort to a loser's post-defeat expiatory comment was given a unanimous approval rating by the group, and is a typical example of a winning verbal strategy:

I am the Master of this game.

Yeah, the Master Bater (winning retort).

Such exchanges are usually curt and blunt. If a player is unable to respond quickly and effectively he will suffer the ridicule and scorn of the audience. Responding slowly is perceived to show a lack of intelligence. Slow responders are frequently called 'morons' and 'idiots.' Rarely do insults go unchallenged, since this kind of passive behaviour would be perceived immediately as highly damaging to one's status.

One of the principal ways in which to prevail in a verbal duel is to make reference in a demeaning fashion to the opponent's family, especially to his mother. The following excerpt is typical of this. Note as well the presence of ELP and CLP features in the dialogue:

(Sarcastically) I like your fucking hair B. It looks like you're in the Jackson 5 for fuck sakes.

Fuck you, mushroom head! Looks like you're wearing a dick on yours.

At least I have a dick B.

Yeah! But it's up your mother's ass.

(Group laughter) Hoo hoo, ya' got rocked R.

Fuck off, assholes.

A verbal duelling strategy that surfaced frequently, and which is also illustrated in the excerpt above, was insulting the opponent's physiological characteristics (hair, penis, height, weight, etc.). Once again, the novelty and force of the insult increased its effectiveness. Previously used verbal ploys were perceived to be ineffectual. A verbal combatant who used an unimaginative ploy was immediately criticized for using something 'cheap' or 'old' – a criticism that surfaced constantly on the tapes.

Insulting the sexual preferences of the opponent was also an effective counter strike tactic employed in duelling exchanges. The members of the clique were particularly sensitive to accusations of homosexuality. An effective repartee in such cases invariably involved an obscenity (often with a homophobic tinge):

What are ya' trying to do, sock me?

Oh yeah, I socked you.

Lick my balls.

May I lick them, badly, or does it hurt that way?

(Group laughter)

Fuck off.

Roll the fucking dice.

I'm just admiring you, okay?

Admiring my penis?

Why would I fucking do that? Are you a homo? (Waits expecting victory.)

We all are R. Don't deny the truth.

(Group laughter)

Fucking sick.

Another finding was that one of the most prestigious qualities a teenage male is expected to possess is the ability to entertain clique members by making them laugh. The member acclaimed as the 'clown prince' of the clique at any given time was always accorded ample verbal time in all kinds of exchanges. As Maltz and Borker (1982: 210) observed, clown prince status is achieved through an adeptness in telling stories and jokes in a jocular and clever manner. To maintain his status, the clown prince must also be able to face and defeat any taunting challenges that the audience puts forward. The following excerpt reveals how various individuals in the clique vied, during one particular conversation, for clown prince status:

Imagine being a referee, maaan.

Yeah right, being a ref ... get sweared at every ten minutes.

Imagine a shark biting you, maaan.

Imagine! Do you know that sharks close their eyes when they bite?

Imagine a snake trying to bite you.

Shit, maaan.

The humour, in this case, was of an analogical nature. The comparison to a referee occurred while the informants were watching a hockey game on television. This stimulated a series of retorts in which analogical references to animals were made. The one most capable of making such retorts humorous was ascribed the status of clown prince at that time. He was, however, constantly challenged thereafter by aspirants to his 'throne.'

Another verbal tactic that emerged from the recordings can be called 'besting.' The objective of this verbal ploy was to recall the most entertaining event – the 'best' event – of some shared experience. The topic was generally a party, a movie, a date, a sports event, and so on. An example follows:

Lets watch Cheech and Chong maaan. That movie's the best.

Yeah, when he says he ate the most hash you've ever seen.

That's the funniest.

I smoked so many things maaan, nothing affects me, ha ha.

The best is when the car's going down the highway.

Oh yeah, when the smoke's coming out.

Oh the best was the concert at the end, maaan.

Yeah, yeah, that's the best.

The one who comes up with the 'best' example of a shared experience is the one who wins out, who literally has 'bested' the others. In the above example, the one who recalled the concert scene was acknowledged as the winner because it was recalled by all group members as the most humorous scene in the movie.

The main finding of this research project has been, arguably, that power is achieved within a male teenage clique primarily through a skilful manipulation of language. The teens who are particularly adept at deploying techniques such as swearing, using the CLP feature effectively (le mot juste), coming up with novel insults in response to verbal challenges, deploying sarcasm and obscene language effectively, keeping their cool vis-à-vis opponent and audience mocking-ploys, having the capacity to employ humour for effect, and knowing how 'to best' in the recall of

shared experiences are the ones who will climb the ladder
of prestige within the clique. The leaders of the clique
were, in fact, the ones who possessed these verbal skills in
greater doses. Prowess at verbal duelling is symbolic power. As Tannen (1990: 139) observes, the strategic use of humour in particular is a characteristic of male teenage talk,
rather than of female conversation, because the telling of
jokes is the male's 'way of negotiating status.' And although the telling of obscene jokes referring to female
anatomy is now a taboo in North American culture, such
jokes, as Barreca (1991: 155) has noted, are 'still staples
among all-male groups.'

**Cross-Cultural Comparisons**

Recently, I conducted a follow-up study on teenage speech
patterns in Italy. The idea was to determine the extent to
which the pubilectal categories posited above were valid
in another cultural setting. With two other investigators
(Diana Competrini and Sofia Papaianni), I recorded spontaneous speech samples of adolescents living in Naples
and attending the Liceo Genovese there. Interviews with
the students were also conducted.

Seventeen students (aged fifteen to seventeen) were
chosen for the study. All three categories were found to
surface in their discourse. ELP was seen in such utterances
as: 'Devo, mmmm, dire che, mmmmm, non capisco,
mmmmmm' = 'I have ... to say that ... I don't understand ...'
with the 'mmmmmm' being equivalent in function to
English 'like.' Rising intonation, exaggerated prosody, and
the like were also found to be typical concomitants of adolescent utterances.

The CLP category was also found to be a highly productive one. A few examples will suffice to illustrate its manifestation in Italian:

• a 'togo' is someone who is 'bello, stupendo, divertente'

('handsome, stupendous, fun to be with'; it is a term roughly equivalent to the English 'cool')

- a 'grasta' is a female teen who is 'cretina, stupida, scema' ('cretin, stupid, jerk'; it is a word equivalent to the English 'loser')

- a 'secchione' is someone who is 'troppo studioso' ('studies too much'; it is equivalent to the English 'dork' or 'nerd').

Eighty-seven such words were recorded during the one-week period spent at this specific school. Ongoing research in several other parts of Italy is producing similar findings. For example, De Paoli (1988) calls the language of Italian adolescents living in Milan, Bologna, and other northern cities and towns 'the language of rock and roll,' so influenced is it by the formulas and modes of speech of Anglo-American rock.

Cross-cultural comparisons are beginning to show, in fact, that pubilectal categories seem to emerge in any culture where teenagerhood constitutes a distinct social category. Through worldwide broadcasts of English-language channels such as MTV, North American models of teenagerhood are being adopted mimetically in many other parts of the world. Data on pubilects throughout the world are beginning to show that teens the world over live in the same kind of symbolic universe. Teenagers live and act in a mind-world created by the particular meta-codes they acquire.

# 5

# The Future of Teenagerhood

*Young people are commercially managed into group identifications, values, and behaviours under the presence of individualized preferences.*
Key (1989: 12)

The motivation behind the observations and commentaries offered so far has been, as I indicated in the preface, to provide a semiotic analysis of what was implicit in the statement 'It's *cool* to be *cool!*' uttered to me by a thirteen-year-old schoolmate of my daughter over a decade ago. *Being cool* for the denizens of the contemporary social territory that I have called *teenagerhood* entails knowing how to dress for a peer audience, how to carve out an appropriate body image for that same audience, what kind of rock music is fashionable, which peers to hang out with, how to smoke, what parties to attend, how to speak in strategic ways, and so on. These are the codes (clique-specific and meta-) that constitute coolness. They are acquired by what I have called signifying osmosis, a process that involves osmotic biological tendencies intersecting with social cognition. An implicit sociological theme that I have attempted to weave throughout my observations and analyses has been that young people have not always been this way, that teenagerhood is a social phenomenon that crystallized at mid century in North American society.

The teenager of today has a recognizable persona and a cultural context which maintains and nurtures it. Rock musicians and prototypes of teens in the media help to define and sustain the style, comportment, and mind-set of the modern teenager. Success at school has become, by and large, an issue of secondary importance for the contemporary teen, at least during the early teen years. Possessing and managing the appropriate symbology of coolness has become his or her primary concern. All this is rather ironic, since the fashioning of the contemporary teen persona has come about by making schooling mandatory to sixteen years of age. It is precisely the high school environment that provides the primary locus within which teens anchor their social lives. It is their school chums with whom they hang out, go to parties, and share symbologies.

Adolescence is a transitional developmental phase which entails culture-specific responses to the physical and emotional changes that characterize it. In our culture these responses have been allowed to cohere into the symbology of teenagerhood. More than ever, teens act and behave in terms of peer-generated codes.

To be sure, the semiotic sketches of the teenage persona in this book are sometimes overdrawn. Not every adolescent aspires to become cool. Indeed, the high schools are filled with adolescents studying hard, striving to achieve well-defined goals, and immune, by and large, to the influence of the teenage subculture and of its requirement to become *cool*. But it is also true to say that *coolness* has become 'symptomatic' of how adolescents develop socially: that is, more and more adolescents are reflecting some aspect of the portrait I have drawn, even if only in approximate ways.

The experience of adolescence cannot help but be highly diversified today in North America, given the high degree of variability in the onset of puberty, the large number of ethnically diverse teens in urban societies, and the socioeconomic heterogeneity of teens living in large cities.

Nonetheless, I believe it is accurate to say that most of the adolescents living in our culture are aware of the characteristics of the portrait I have sketched, and that at various points in their adolescent development they have manifested some of its features.

In this concluding chapter, I will offer my final observations on the phenomenon of teenagerhood. I will first look at teenagers and the media and comment one last time on the role of the high school in the social engineering of teenagerhood. Then, I will discuss the mythology of childhood vis-à-vis the new mythology of teenagerhood. Finally, I will give my own 'semiotic prognostications' on what the world inhabited by the post-modern ('post-post-modern'?) teenager will be like.

### Teenagers and the Media

Is the media the shaper of behaviour that many would claim it is today? Have television and radio generated teenagerhood? Are teenagers victims of the media, as Key (1989: 13) suggests, observable 'as they scream and shout hysterically at rock concerts and later in life at religious revival meetings'?

Key is, in large part, correct in emphasizing the role that the media play in shaping behaviours in individuals. The constantly increasing consumption of fast food, alcohol, and other media-hyped substances among teens is no doubt influenced to some degree by television advertising. And, indeed, it may also be partially true that television imparts models of behaviour. As Strasburger (1993: 173) puts it: 'TV offers kids "scripts" about gender roles, conflict resolution, and patterns of courtship and sexual gratification that they may not be able to observe anywhere else.' But, in my view, any influence that television has on teens is of a mimetic nature. It is not as powerful a shaper of their behaviours as is signifying osmosis. Even though they mindlessly absorb the messages promulgated constantly by TV programming and commercials, and although these may have some subliminal effects on their behaviour, today's teens are affected by media images mainly if they reflect or reinforce already established clique-based behaviours. It is my view that teenagers are influenced primarily by peer osmosis. It is, in fact, peers who influence a teen to watch certain programs, to buy certain rock tapes or videos, and so on. Peer osmosis is a much more powerful shaper of the teenage persona than is media mimesis. In my opinion, it is more accurate to say that television produces programs and images for teens that reinforce already forged models of coolness. Media moguls are more intent on extracting the models already inherent in teen behaviours and reinforcing them than in spreading innovations. In the fifties, teens watched 'American Bandstand,' a program which was pivotal in imparting meta-codes (musical preferences, fashions, hairstyles, etc.). But this dance program did no more than reflect what the teens were already predisposed to model. As Goodwin (1992: 187) points out, even contemporary programs like MTV are not in themselves disruptive of the value systems of the cultural mainstream; rather, they reflect 'shifts' already present in the popular culture.

Nevertheless, I realize that the role of television in contemporary culture cannot be underestimated. By the late thirties television service was in place in several Western countries. The British BBC, for example, started a regular service in 1936. By the early forties there were twenty-three television stations operating in the United States. But it was not until the early fifties that technology had advanced to the point where it was possible for virtually every North American household to afford a television set. Almost immediately, television personalities became household names, mythologized into 'deities' who loomed larger than life. Actors and announcers became celebrities. People began to plan their daily lives more and more around television programs, waiting anxiously for their favourite shows to come on the air. I can still remember the enthusiasm with which the 'Ed Sullivan Show' on Sunday evenings was anticipated in the fifties and early sixties. Performers like Elvis Presley and the Beatles became instant mythic heroes after only one appearance on the show. By the early seventies television had become much more than just a technologically advanced *medium* of entertainment. Today, television is blamed for causing virtually everything, from obesity to street violence.

Throughout the fifties and sixties, television programming developed rapidly into what it is today – a *social text* geared to the daily viewing habits of an increasingly larger and larger segment of society. Today, 98 per cent of North American households own a television set, and a large portion of these have more than one. Through advances in satellite communications, we can now even perceive ourselves as 'participants' in wars and conflicts going on in some other part of the world. Indeed, these days most of our information, intellectual stimulation, entertainment, and lifestyle models come from, or are related to, the television text. People have become dependent on television in much the same way a drug addict is on some chemical substance. Psychological studies are constantly pointing out that people who are deprived of their daily dose of television display the same 'withdrawal-like symptoms' addicts do.

As the great Canadian communications theorist Marshall McLuhan (e.g., 1962, 1964) pointed out, the *medium* in the case of television has become the *message*. I do believe, therefore, that it does have effects on cognition. But these are not limited to teens. There are three kinds of effects whose manifestations are easily detectable in the population at large. I will refer to these as the *mythologizing effect*, the *event fabrication effect*, and the *information compression effect*.

By mythologizing effect I am referring to the fact that television imbues its personages with a mythological aura.

Like any type of privileged space – a platform, pulpit, or any other specially constructed locus that is designed to impart focus and significance to someone – television creates mythic heroes by simply 'containing' them. Media personalities of all types are infused with a deified quality by virtue of the fact that they are 'seen' inside the mythical space created by television.

By event fabrication effect I am referring to the perceptual state that television induces in its viewers as it transforms some ordinary happening into a momentous *event* – an election campaign, an actor's love affair, a fashion trend, and so on. People make up their minds about the guilt or innocence of someone by watching '60 Minutes'; they come to see certain behaviours as laudable or damnable by tuning into 'Oprah' or 'Geraldo'; they experience the moral sentiments of rectitude and justice by viewing the capturing of some criminal on 'Cops.' A riot that gets airtime becomes a momentous event; one that does not is ignored. This is why terrorists are seemingly more interested in simply 'getting on the air' than in having their demands satisfied. The mere fact of being on television imbues their cause with event status and, therefore, with significance. Political and social protesters frequently inform the news media of their intentions, and then dramatically stage their demonstrations in front of the cameras. Sports events like the World Series, the Super Bowl, or the Stanley Cup playoffs are transformed on television into herculean struggles. Events such as the John F. Kennedy and Lee Harvey Oswald assassinations, the Vietnam War, the Watergate hearings, the Rodney King beating, and the like are transformed into portentous and prophetic historical events, similar to the great classical dramas and their import for ancient cultures. It is probably no great exaggeration to suggest that television has become the *maker* of history and its *documenter* at the same time. Television is how people now *experience* history; and, conversely, television is also *shaping* history. The horrific scenes coming out of the Vietnam War and transmitted into people's homes every day in the late sixties and early seventies had significant military and social consequences. More recently, one thinks of the incredible image of an MTV flag being hoisted by East German youths over the Berlin Wall as it was being torn down. And, as Andersson (1990: 233) has remarked, it is amazing to contemplate that, according to 'trivia-keepers, more people watched the wedding of England's Prince Charles and Princess Diana than had ever before in human history observed such an event at the same time,' and that many international events were postponed one year, at the height of the popularity of 'Dallas,' simply because people 'wanted to stay around and find out who shot J.R. Ewing!'

By information compression effect I am referring to the fact that the medium of television presents events, information, and so on, globally and instantly, leaving little time for one to reflect on their implications. This information compression effect has created a new way in which to perceive messages and their meanings. Collectively, we have developed a short attention span that requires constant variety in information content. It is as if we have become so habituated to large doses of information, cut up, packaged, and pre-digested, that we have developed a psychological dependence on information and visual stimulation. This effect is, in my view, the reason why television is vastly more popular than reading for many teens. It is an arduous task for a teen to read a book in the evenings after work or school, since its form and content must be decoded at various levels of cognition. The reading process thus causes a slowdown in the intake of information. TV viewing, on the other hand, is very easy to do. During a news broadcast, for instance, the items, film footage, and commentaries are all fast-paced and brief. They are designed to be visually dramatic snippets of easily digestible information. 'Within such a stylistic environment,' writes Stuart Ewen (1988: 265), 'the news is beyond comprehension.' The facts of the news are subjected to the stylized signature of the specific news program – the same story will be interpreted differently according to whoever the television journalist is. As Ewen (265–6) aptly puts it: 'Nations and people are daily sorted out into boxes marked "good guys," "villains," "victims," and "lucky ones," style becomes the essence, reality becomes the appearance.'

A technical innovation of the last decade has entrenched the information compression effect into our cultural mindset even more deeply: the remote control. Actually, this device was invented in 1956 by a man named Robert Adler. But it wasn't until the eighties that it became a standard prop of virtually every television set. The remote control has had an enormous impact on how we view television. More significantly, it has made the further compression of information a reality. When we are bored with something on a specific channel, all we have to do from the comfort of our viewing seats is to flick through the panoply of viewing options at our disposal, rapidly and with very little deliberation or reflection. We seek instant gratification and control with this versatile little device. Whoever holds the remote control during family viewing sessions is also the one who has implicit control over the others.

So, I too believe that television has an influence on teens. But that influence is not the one that some psychologists talk about. What I have called the mythologizing, event fabrication, and information compression effects do indeed influence the cognitive processing of information. But they do not induce aberrant or violent behaviours. The greatest source of behavioural influence on teens comes from peer interactions.

### The High School

There is no doubt in my mind that the high schools (and junior highs) that North American adolescents are required to attend provide the contexts in which clique-based behaviours are formed and allowed to run their course. The high school has become the primary locus for teen socialization, and it is here where signifying osmosis induces the behavioural codes that constitute coolness. But, it is also fair to say that not all adolescents see the school as a social universe. As Eckert (1988: 188) observes, although the majority of teens 'center their lives around the school and its activities,' there are 'those who reject the hegemony of the school' altogether. The latter are the many runaways and street kids who now populate the downtown cores of major urban areas. These kids develop a 'streetwise' form of teenagerhood and coolness.

The high school environment provided a social cosmos for fifties teens. But the primary focus of the school day then was academic. Socialization rituals took place primarily outside of school hours. But more and more, the high school is becoming the primary focal point for establishing and maintaining peer relations. Academic achievement is of less importance, at least till the later grades. But even then, students typically perceive their final years in high school as a last attempt to achieve a peak level in social status, both within a specific clique and within the high school community at large, before academic or job-related interests become dominant.

The high school is where friendships are forged, clique allegiances established, conflictual behaviours between teens and cliques developed, social personalities manufactured, and so on. The school is a closed social system. Newcomers must pass initiation rites; outsiders are looked upon with suspicion and must be introduced into the school by a school member; losers are marginalized. Sex and violence are learned here, where they are real! There would be no teenagerhood without high schools.

## The Mythology of Childhood

Teenagerhood can be said to constitute a mythology, in the

same way that childhood does. As discussed in the opening chapter, categories such as childhood and adolescence
reflect the ways in which cultures perceive biologically
significant periods in the life cycle. In other words, such
categories are attempts to relate our biological heritage to
communal sense-making.

Once cultures segment the life cycle into such categories
there is a tendency to associate idealized, prototypical
characteristics with those whom the categories are meant
to represent. These cohere into mythologies, each with
themes and motifs that are felt to express significant truths
about human life. Periods in life are, in fact, perceived to
constitute stories. The details of the telling change from
context to context, just as stories do. It would be no exaggeration, in fact, to say that the mind seems to have a 'narrative' structure that manifests itself extrinsically in the
form of the stories, myths, and mythologies that all individuals and cultures invariably create.

The study of how mythical narratives describe and portray the origin and basic experiences of a culture is probably as old as civilization itself. In ancient Greece there
emerged a debate over myth and story-making vs. reason,
or *logos*, as a reliable means for looking at what was happening and what was going to happen in the world. Xeno-
phanes, Plato, and Aristotle, for example, trenchantly
criticized myths as symbolic tools for explaining reality,
instead exalting reason as the only trustworthy means for
gaining access to the outer world of reality and the inner
world of human experience. But the ancient debate, and
the advent of the rational scientific method, did not elim-
inate the need for story-making in human civilization. On
the contrary, throughout history there has always been a
propensity to produce and rely on narrative accounts – factual and fictional – to explain who we are and why we are
here. Even in the domains of inquiry that we call 'science'
or 'technology,' there is (and probably has always been) a
deeply felt suspicion that the narrative mode of explana-

tion plays a fundamental role in constructing the whole edifice of rational science.

According to Roland Barthes (1957), cultural mythologies such as childhood are reflexes of mythic thinking. Childhood connotes 'innocence'; old age, 'wisdom.' In early Hollywood westerns, for instance, the mythic 'good' vs. 'evil' dichotomy was portrayed by having the heroes wear white and the villains black. Sports events are mythical dramas juxtaposing the 'good' (the hometown hero or team) vs. the 'bad' (the outsider or visiting team). The whole fanfare associated with preparing for the 'big event,' like the World Series of baseball or the Superbowl of American football, has a ritualistic quality similar to the pomp and circumstance that ancient armies engaged in before going out to battle and war. Indeed, the whole event is perceived to be a mythic battle. The symbolism of the 'home' team's (the army's) uniform, the 'valour' and 'strength' of star players (the heroic warriors), and the capacities of the coach (the army general) all have a profound emotional effect on the fans (one of the two warring nations). The game (the battle) is perceived to unfold in moral terms: it is the struggle of the forces of 'righteousness' and 'beauty' against the forces of 'ugliness' and 'baseness.' Sports figures are exalted as heroes or condemned as villains. Victory is interpreted in moral terms as a struggle of good vs. evil. The game is, as the television and radio ads constantly blurt out, 'real life, real drama!'

Mythologies have, clearly, great emotional power in all cultures. Without them, cultures would be limited virtually to carrying out only survival functions at a rudimentary level. Sports events replace great battles, spectacles reenact our need for ritual and dramatic performance, sweet-sixteen birthday parties signal a 'rite of passage,' and the list could go on and on. The human-made world is a mythological one.

Childhood was forged as a mythology during the Romantic movement, when goodness, love, and justice were attributed to humans uncorrupted and untainted by civilization. These 'noble savages' were purported to be the 'children' of humanity. Such views did not exist in previous eras, nor are they found to be universal even today. In medieval and Renaissance paintings and portraits there are no 'children,' at least not in the way we think of them. The 'babes' and 'children' that do appear occasionally in such portraits look more like miniature adults than children.

Before the Industrial Revolution of the nineteenth century, most people lived in agricultural communities or settings. Children barely out of infancy were expected to help with the farm. There was, consequently, little distinction between childhood and adult roles – children were perceived, apparently, to be adults with smaller and weaker bodies. During the Industrial Revolution the centre of economic activity shifted from the farm to the city, which forced many people to move into the city (urbanization). This urbanization also led to the construction of a new social order with different role categories and assignments. The result was that children were left with few of their previous responsibilities, and a new mythology emerged, one which saw children as vastly different from adults, needing the time to learn at school, to play, and so on. Child labour laws were passed and public education became compulsory. Protected from the harsh reality of industrial work, children came to assume a new, pristine identity as innocent, faultless, impressionable, malleable organisms. To this day, we think of children as living in some Disney-type world, in some 'Fantasyland.'

As Marshall (1992: 10–11) has also pointed out, prior to the nineteenth century

children, let alone teenagers, were not seen as a distinct group. They were viewed as mini-adults who were expected to behave as such as soon as possible. For example, crawling was not seen as the milestone it is today. Rather, the sight of one's offspring crawling on the floor was more likely to be viewed as animal-like behavior that should be promptly corrected. Special clothes were even designed that kept children in a rigid, adult-like posture as soon as they were able to stand.

Lawrence Grossberg (1992: 171) extends this analysis to the notion of youth generally:

The meaning of youth is, and must remain, uncertain. It is not merely a question of the historical construction of the category, nor of its ambiguous relation to other categories preceding adulthood (childhood, adolescence, 'young adulthood'). It is not merely that the referent of youth is a site for struggle; for the very register of that reference is itself constantly at stake. Youth can be a matter of chronology, sociology, ideology, experience, style, attitude.

Children are no more than younger human beings undergoing growth in body, mind, and personality. They are *different* from adults, not any better or worse. The images of children as 'pure,' 'innocent,' and so on, are part of a mythology, not a psychology or sociology of childhood. A child has no awareness whatsoever of being pure or innocent until he or she is so informed.

Perhaps, as Helen Fisher (1992: 233) suggests, the mythology of childhood has come about because, unlike other primates, humans 'continue to rear their offspring some ten to twelve years after these children have been weaned.' As a consequence, human childhood has become 'almost twice as long as that of chimps and other primates.'

Childhood has, consequently, generated its own symbolic order. Consider why we give toys to children. Recall what happened during the 1983 Christmas shopping season (see Solomon 1988: 77–93). That was the period of the 'Cabbage Patch Doll' craze. Hordes of parents were prepared to pay almost anything to get one of those dolls for their daughters. Scalpers offered the suddenly and unexplainably 'out-of-stock' dolls (a marketing ploy?) for hundreds of dollars through the classified ads. Grown adults fought each other in line-ups to get one of the few remaining dolls left in stock at some toy outlet.

How could a toy, a simple doll, have caused such mass hysteria? To a semiotician, only something with great mythological signification could have possibly triggered such intense commotion. To see why this is so, let us investigate the semiotic nature of toys. Why do we give toys to our children at all? What sorts of toys do we give them and why?

Consider, for example, the humanoid toys we give our children – dolls and action hero toys. It is interesting to note that the Cabbage Patch dolls came with 'adoption papers.' This is a concrete clue as to what the dolls really signified. Each doll was given a name – taken at random from 1938 state of Georgia birth records – which, like any act of naming, conferred upon it a personality and human reality. And, thanks to computerized factories, no two dolls were alike. The doll became alive in the child's mind, as do all objects with names. The dolls provided the precious human contact that children living in modern nuclear families where the parents or guardians work desperately need. Dolls are 'people substitutes.' In some cultures, one is purported to be able to have some physical or psychological effect on a person by doing something to a doll constructed to resemble them. In our culture, children 'talk' to their dolls. These invariably are felt to 'lend a receptive ear' to their owners' needs and frustrations. Dolls answer a deep need for human contact. No wonder, then, that the Cabbage Patch episode was such a hysterical one. Parents were not buying a simple doll; in effect, they were buying their child a sibling.

The idea of giving toys fits in rather nicely with the mythology of childhood. Children have always 'played' with objects. Objects take on signification in any way we wish to assign it to them: broom handles can become swords, rocks can be thought of as balls, and so on. Objects with memory value (e.g., objects given as gifts from some loved one) have great signifying power. If they are somehow 'misplaced' (e.g., taken away from a bedroom), the result can be literally 'felt' as a personal violation. This is because our persona is projected into our objects. They are extensions of ourselves. Toys, as the name of a major North American toystore chain states, are indeed us (Toys R Us). We give toys to children as we would give ourselves. In many ways, this act of giving soothes our sense of guilt for not being able to be with our children more often. We give them toys because we have no time to give ourselves to them. Moreover, the *type* of toy we give is synchronized to any mythology of gender that is in place at the time of giving: a few years ago, little girls were given Barbie dolls and little boys Rambo dolls in order to keep the gender dichotomy between males and females operative. Barbie dolls connoted our culture-specific view of femininity (passiveness, preoccupation with physical appearance, etc.), while Rambo toys connoted our views of masculinity (aggressiveness, toughness, patriotism, etc.). As our mythologies of gender and childhood have now changed, so too do the toys we give to children. There is no question that the signifying value of toys will change again. Such is the nature of human culture.

## The New Mythology of Teenagerhood

Between 1946 and 1964 a baby boom took place in North America whose magnitude had no precedent. During that period, seventy-seven million babies were born (Grossberg 1992: 172). No wonder, then, that the fifties saw a juvenilization of culture and the emergence of a teenage subculture. By 1957 the new teenage consumer market was worth over thirty billion dollars a year (173). Teenagerhood was in large part constructed and institutionalized by the exigencies of the post–Second World War economy.

Predictably, the formation of a new social category on the biological continuum has entailed its own mythology. Teenagers are now assumed to act, think, and behave in specific ways. This mythology has been constructed by adults and reinforced by adult institutions like television, not by the teens themselves. Teens are just as unaware of their mythology as children are of theirs. Fifties television programs such as 'The Adventures of Ozzie and Harriet' sculpted the teenage persona to fit the emerging new mythology. This persona had a new body, a new behavioural code, and a new set of aesthetic tastes. In the sixties, teenagers in media portrayals became 'older' and more socially-committed. The mythology had changed somewhat to fit new realities. Today, the teen in programs like 'Beverly Hills, 90210' has reacquired some of the traits of fifties teen prototypes. But the contemporary post-modern world is not so simple. The rosy-coloured family relations in 'Ozzie and Harriet' have degenerated into the macabre, senseless, actions parodied for the sake of parody in 'Married ... with Children.' The father on this program, Al Bundy, has been totally deconstructed. He is a reprehensible character who just happens to be 'married' and who just happens to have 'children,' children who are just as shallow and despicable as he is. Al Bundy, a throwback to Ralph Kramden of the 'Honeymooners' and Archie Bunker of 'All in the Family,' is the end result of the deconstruction of the baby-boomer father symbol on television. He is the opposite of wise and judicious TV dads like Jim Anderson of 'Father Knows Best' or Bill Cosby of 'The Cosby Show.' Al Bundy is a fifties ex-teenager who still yearns for his own particular brand of teenagerhood.

'Married ... with Children' requires further commentary here. It is indeed a 'deconstructive' parody – a scathing mimicry of traditional family values and roles. 'Al Bundy is the father figure as he really is,' the show blurts out. The television programs of the fifties and sixties had built up an idyllic mythology of fatherhood. Even the titles of the shows – 'Father Knows Best,' 'Life with Father' – clearly revealed a mythology based on patriarchy and paternal authority within the family. This patriarchal mythology began to be challenged in the late sixties and throughout the seventies and eighties by programs such as 'The Mary Tyler Moore Show,' 'Rhoda,' 'Maude,' 'The Days and Nights of Molly Dodd,' 'Cagney and Lacey,' 'Kate and Allie' and others which portrayed strong, independent women who were attempting to survive, socially and professionally, in a world that was deconstructing patriarchal structures. Women were achieving a new image and status, and men were being increasingly relegated to an Archie Bunker–type status as anti-heroes. Al Bundy is a downtrodden boor who has all the wrong answers to family problems, and who always feels sorry for himself. His wife, Peggy, sports a moronic hairdo and is constantly struggling to make Al more sexually interested in her. Bud Bundy, his teenage son, is a loser. His sister, Kelly, is ignorant and interested only in sex. There is no sugar-coating here. The Bundys are caricatures of what is traditional in television family shows – warmth, moral rectitude, success, and high ideals. They are boorish, inept, unsuccessful, vulgar, and cynical. There are many social messages coming out of this program. But above all else, it satirizes parents who base their love on their children's accomplishments; it critiques male chauvinism and child exploitation; and it satirizes sex relations and society's views on female sexuality.

It is interesting to note that in the midst of this mythological deconstruction, a show like 'The Cosby Show' achieved unexpected success throughout the eighties. There were a number of reasons for the success of this apparent throwback to the patriarchal programs of the fifties and sixties. First and foremost is the fact the Bill Cosby himself is a true comedian who can easily endear himself to a large audience. But, more important, 'The Cosby Show' was appropriate for the eighties. Throughout the seventies, programs like 'All in the Family' and 'The Jeffersons' were products of an iconoclastic movement to tear down all kinds of authority models and figures. But during the eighties, with the ascendancy of a new right-wing moralism, as evidenced by the election of conservative governments in Canada and the United States (Mulroney, Reagan, Bush), the myth of patriarchal authority was making a kind of comeback. Once more, audiences were searching for TV father-figures who were both strong and understanding. Bill Cosby fit this image perfectly. Bill Cosby is our culture's idealization of what a father should be like. He is a success story. The only real difference between Bill Cosby and Jim Anderson of 'Father Knows Best' is the fact that Cosby's wife, unlike Anderson's, played a different, more assertive role within the revamped mythology of patriarchy. The family scene on 'The Cosby Show' reflected what a tightly knit, successful family should look like. It provided a symbol of reassurance and faith in traditional values in a world that was, and continues to be, in constant moral doubt and flux.

Al Bundy is a parody of those who still live in what can be called 'the Elvis culture.' People invariably recall with amazing detail their affectively coded teen experiences (the first kiss, party incidents, etc.); they remain tenaciously attached to the songs and rock stars of their era; they continue to dress and groom themselves as they did when they were teens. There is, of course, nothing particularly revealing about this. Great writers from all eras have written extensively about 'first love' and other early life experiences. But the cultural gestalt of such feeling structures has changed. The reverence for Elvis Presley that the fifties generation of 'ex-teens' continues to have is a case in point. Presley died on 16 August 1977. Since then, there have been constant pilgrimages to his house; his records and movies (in video form) are being continually reissued; and many fans even keep shrines and relics (vials of his sweat, scraps of carpet from his house, etc.) in their homes. Recently, Elvis was immortalized on a US stamp. It is both humorous and disconcerting to contemplate how powerful teenagerhood has become emotionally, and how indelible an imprint it leaves on memory and personality.

Today, many middle-aged parents are experiencing a hard time accepting the new behavioural models of their teens. On the one hand, there is good reason for their dismay and apprehension. Drug and alcohol consumption, partying, smoking, and so on, have become fixtures of the cool lifestyle of contemporary teens. On the other hand, it seems to me that many contemporary adults frequently find themselves in confrontational situations with their teenage sons or daughters because they do not see a discontinuity between themselves and their children. Many parents today do not see themselves, as do adults in primitive tribes, as elders preparing to become wise for the benefit of their culture and their youth. The effacement of the boundary line between young and old is being nurtured by vested economic interests. Al Bundy is the symbol of this ultimately deleterious trend in our culture.

As mentioned at the beginning of this chapter, I believe that it is unlikely that young people are the primary victims of television, as some psychologists would claim. Children and teens are more influenced by their families and by their peers than they are by media images. In my opinion, there is no causal link between television violence, for instance, and violence in society in general. Did television engender the wars fought throughout history, including the two devastating world wars of this century? Did it spur Jack the Ripper to slash his victims to death? Of course it didn't; it didn't exist. In their authoritative 1988 study of the effects of television on children and adolescents, Liebert and Sprafkin showed that there was a tenuous link between aggressiveness in children and watching violent television; but, they also showed that television is only one factor in this increased behavioural pattern, not *the* cause, and that its effects were extremely short-lasting.

There is no one cause of aggressive behaviour in children. What is more accurate to say is that the general *modus pensandi* and the behavioural models of our culture are reflected in the television text. But, as programs like 'Married ... with Children' reveal, this text is always subject to criticism and ultimately to change. Social texts are made by people and, therefore, they reflect what people think and want.

In the twenties, the anthropologist Margaret Mead could feel that a new mythology was taking shape in North America. So she set out to show that the views of adolescence as a *Sturm und Drang* period, characterized by a need to overcome fear of self and solitude by submission to some self-chosen leader and by open contumacious displays of rebellion against any and every authority, were culture-specific. Her work among the preliterate peoples on the island of Samoa (e.g., Mead 1939, 1950) showed that in such societies puberty signalled entry into the social mainstream, not a period of protracted and encouraged psychosocial adjustment. As Mead described it, the growth of female Samoan adolescents was continuous and smooth, not interrupted and jagged. The young Samoan girl assumed her new role in the world by assisting in adult activities – caring for children, catching fish, cleaning house, participating in dances and rituals. Boys and girls engaged freely in courtships at puberty without any intimations of guilt or shame. Mead (1939: 157) painted the following portrait of Samoan adolescence:

Adolescence represented no period of crisis or stress but was instead an orderly developing of a set of slowly maturing interests and activities. The girls' minds were perplexed by no conflicts, troubled by no philosophical queries, beset by no remote ambitions. To live as a girl with many lovers as long as possible, and then marry in one's own village, near one's own relatives, and to have many children, these were uniform and satisfying ambitions.

These words were written well in advance of Holden Caulfield's moral angst and the crystallization of a teen subculture in the fifties. One wonders what Mead would have to say today about the post-modern teenager and the mythology that teenagerhood now entails. In Samoa there was no preoccupation with body image, no preoccupation and paranoia over sex and identity. As a consequence, smoking rituals, partying, hanging-out, and all the other traits of the Western teenager simply could not emerge in the Samoan culture of the twenties and thirties.

What are some of the most pervasive and entrenched assumptions vis-à-vis teenagerhood? First and foremost, there is the belief that it is inevitable. But, as discussed above, Margaret Mead has shown us the untenability of this assumption.

Second, it is widely thought that teens know more than enough about sex. Despite explicit sexuality in the media, however, teens actually know very little about sex. And what they do know, they pick up osmotically from peers. The tapes I recorded to examine pubilect (and discussed in the previous chapter) revealed to me that teens of both genders continually 'teach' each other, in their own idiosyncratic ways, about the allure and pleasures of sex. Teens do not pick up their notions of sex mimetically from the media, but osmotically from peer interaction. It is the peer-based symbology of sex that both *forms* and *informs* them.

The third common assumption is that teens are idealistic, Caulfieldian-like dreamers. But the most common pattern I discerned over a decade of participant observation was hardly the search for Utopia. Contemporary teens tend to seek the shelter of the clique, not to pursue a Siddhartha-like path to knowledge and wisdom. But the sheltering functions of the clique now entail a risk. Since cliquing is based on an 'all for one, one for all' philosophy, clique conformity often degenerates into a kind of violent mob rule that resembles the actions of many species of birds who attack their prey in mobs. The excitement among such species of attacking the victim is contagious. Even if the victim escapes, the mob members have become so aroused that 'they will go on mobbing for a long while afterwards, as though they cannot calm down to a normal level of activity until some considerable time has passed' (Morris 1990: 90). Over the years, I was a witness several times to instances of mobbing behaviour and gang warfare between teen cliques that truly alarmed and unsettled me. Swarming, ganging up, and so forth, are common features in the animal world – ground squirrels will gang up on snakes from time to time; breeding sea birds will gang up on a fox; chimpanzees will mob a leopard; and so on. But animals do this for one simple reason – survival. Violence in the animal world is never gratuitous. But the violence of teen cliques, as depicted masterfully in the movie *Clockwork Orange* over twenty years ago, is random, senseless violence.

But despite such aberrant behavioural tendencies, I also noticed that they are short-lived, especially as teen cliques develop beyond Dunphy's (1963) second and third stages (see chapter two) and become increasingly heterosexual. Teens do not bond permanently with their peers, and they do not break their family bonds irreparably. As a matter of fact, conflicts often develop among teens within cliques. The intensity of in-clique conflicts is rather startling. Clearly, the emotional attachment one forms with peers can be transformed quickly and dramatically into its opposite.

### The World of the Post-modern Teenager: *Catcher in the Rye* or *Clockwork Orange*?

Holden Caulfield was one of the first fictional teen proto-types. So were the Ackleys and Stradlaters that he described so colourfully. Holden's indictment of society was a strong one. But Holden's denunciation pales in comparison to Alex's violent rejection of the world order in Stanley Kubrick's 1971 cinematic masterpiece, *A Clockwork Orange*.

The setting for the movie is Britain in the near future. A teenage thug, Alex De Large, perpetrates a daily routine of crime and sex in a wanton and reckless fashion. Caught and imprisoned for murder, he volunteers to undergo an experimental shock-treatment therapy, which causes him to become nauseated by his previous lifestyle. Mr Alexander, an author and one of Alex's victims, traps him with the aim of avenging himself. He hopes, sardonically, to drive Alex to commit suicide to the strains of Beethoven's Ninth Symphony. But Alex is supported by the press and soon after he is released and restored to health.

The movie ends in typical post-modern fashion with no true conclusion. But the scenario of senseless, aimless violence perpetrated by a teenager has a profound warning in it. Alex is a portrait of a goal-less and ruthless teen trapped in a weary, decaying environment. His only way out is through intimidation and physical brutality. He is a time-bomb, ready to explode at any instant. Alex, like Holden, feels an acute and urgent need to change – indeed to 'save' – the world. But unlike Holden he does it in a physically destructive manner. The rage in Alex's eyes is the rage shown by contemporary street thugs.

What has gone wrong? Are we living in the worlds depicted by *Catcher in the Rye* and *A Clockwork Orange*? Are Holden Caulfield and Alex De Large really so different? Holden's denunciation is that of a middle-class preppy; Alex's is that of a streetwise gang leader. But both want to 'change the world.'

The work of Lawrence Kohlberg (e.g., 1969, 1978) on the development of moral thought among adolescents is relevant to the present discussion. His work has shown there are three levels at which moral dilemmas are solved by individuals. At the 'preconventional' level, an individual applies cultural standards of right and wrong to the external and physical happenings of a dilemma – 'Should he or she have done it?' – without analysing their meaning. At the 'conventional' level, the individual values group expectations and standards in resolving the dilemma. He or she conforms to these standards and applies them actively to the resolution process. At the 'postconventional' level, the group is no longer paramount in resolving moral dilemmas. Individuals define values apart from their membership in a group.

Kohlberg found that adolescents from thirteen to twenty typically think about moral issues at the conventional level. If Kohlberg is right, then Holden Caulfield constitutes an exception, since he is totally scornful of what his peers think. Alex, on the other hand, is a group leader who can easily persuade those who 'join him' to act upon his desires. He is the one who determines the conventional morality of the streets. As Kohlberg found, North American adolescence is a paradoxical time indeed, a time for simultaneously building and challenging models of morality.

Who will be successful in changing the world order, the Holden Caulfields or the Alex De Larges? In my view, the answer to this rhetorical question is irrelevant, because changing the world order would imply, first and foremost, eliminating teenagerhood itself. And this, in my view, now constitutes a gargantuan task, not only because of the dire economic implications it would have, but also because of the power that teenagerhood holds over cognition and behaviour. Moreover, as mentioned above, the distinction between young and old is becoming less and less obvious. As Stern and Stern (1992: 513) remark, the phenomenal commercial success of the *Teenage Mutant Ninja Turtle* movies and of their associated paraphernalia (comics, toys, etc.), can only be explained as a marketing ploy that was aimed at the parents, and, in turn, their children:

From the beginning, the Turtles were designed with layers of meaning aimed at adults, or at least adolescents, beyond the kiddie market. Their big success among the very young is a good illustration of how energetically pop culture has overrun the lines that once separated children from adults. Just as many modern grown-ups enjoy rock music, goofy T-shirts, comic book collecting, and such major motion-picture-superheros as Batman, Superman, and Dick Tracy (all once considered strictly kid stuff) ... No doubt about it: The turtles are a children's thing; it's just that childhood isn't as childish as it used to be, and adulthood tends to be a lot less mature.

As novelist Douglas Coupland has so persuasively demonstrated in his novel *Generation X* (1991), many of today's identity-less, unmotivated young adults have nowhere to go and nothing to conquer. They feel that they live in a society without goals, a society facing the constant threat of AIDS, child abuse, wife abuse, rape, cancer, divorce, unemployment, and job dissatisfaction. As the narrator of *Generation X* says of himself and his friends, 'We live small lives on the periphery; we are marginalized and there's a great deal in which we choose not to participate' (Coupland 11).

Perhaps, the problem with the post-modern teenager is precisely *that* – that he or she is often victimized by the rampant nihilism of our times and the 'danger of the streets.' The decade I spent studying the semiotics of adolescence forced me to reflect often on this issue. Parents frequently told me that they felt like prisoners in their own homes, slaves to the whims of their teens, but that they preferred this to their sons or daughters leaving home to face the danger of the streets. And their fears are not unfounded: the suicide rate among teens has tripled since 1950; a million teens run away from home every year; the teen homicide rate has increased by 232 per cent since 1950; each year, one million teenage girls become pregnant; the rate of substance abuse has doubled in the last decade; 20 per cent of teenagers are alcoholics (Grossberg 1992: 187).

I conclude by suggesting an answer to a question a harried parent once posed to me after a typical confrontation with his teenage daughter. He asked: 'What can I do to change things?' His question actually contained the answer. If the world is to change, then the process must start 'from the top down.' As Grossberg (184) observes, 'the baby boomers won't let go of youth ... actively resisting and even erasing the generations which might more justifiably claim "youth" as their own.' It is unwise, in my view, to cling on so tenaciously to one's youth.

But perhaps the process of change has already started. Newspaper and magazine articles increasingly are beginning to question the sagacity of allowing the high school environment to function as a locus for socialization and the wisdom of the trend towards continually 'empowering' teens. 'Encouragement' not 'empowerment' is slowly becoming the battle-cry in the media. How successful we will be in 'changing things' remains, however, largely to be seen. Anyone who studies adolescence will soon discover, as I did, that it is a study in contrast, change, experimentation with life, and above all else, growth. Negative perceptions of young people have existed from time immemorial. In the eighth century BC, Hesiod saw no future for society if it was to bequeath its traditions to 'the frivolous youth of today, for certainly all youth are reckless beyond words' (quoted in Rice 1990: 3). So, in one way, today's preoccupation with young people is not much different from what it has always been.

Teenagerhood is symbology. Changing the symbology will change the mind-set. And, I cannot but agree with Grace and Fred Hechinger, who, already in 1963, saw the danger that this symbology entailed: 'American civilization tends to stand in such awe of its teenage segment that it is in danger of becoming a teenage society, with permanently teenage standards of thought, culture, and goals. As a result American society is growing down rather than up' (x).

The juvenilization of culture is the consequence of teenagerhood having been around for four decades. The signs are there for everyone to see. Rock music has become *the* major diversion for society at large; the style and content of movies and television programs are anchored in teenagerhood; fashions of all kinds pass quickly from the teenage to the mainstream culture. But there are also signs that things are likely to change. Today's teen is what Doherty (1988: 237) aptly calls 'a hapless kid seeking direction, not a tough rebel fleeing restriction.' Movies such as *Star Wars* (1977), *The Karate Kid* (1984), and others have come forward to indicate that children and teens need to seek out aged mentors, instruction, discipline, obedience, and aspiration to ideals that transcend the materialistic and the hedonistic. The extended adolescence that has besieged Western society from the fifties onwards, inhibiting the development of a mature society, may come to an end on its own.

# References

Adelman, C. (1976). 'The Language of Teenage Groups.' In *They Don't Speak Our Language*, ed. S. Rogers, 80–105. London: Edward Arnold.

Aitken, P.P. (1980). 'Peer Pressure, Parental Controls and Cigarette Smoking among 10 to 14 Year Olds.' *British Journal of Social and Clinical Psychology* 19: 141–6.

Anderson, W.T. (1992). *Reality Isn't What It Used to Be*. San Francisco: Harper Collins.

Andersson, L., and P. Trudgill. (1990). *Bad Language*. London: Blackwell.

Austin, J.L. (1962). *How to Do Things with Words*. Cambridge, Mass.: Harvard University Press.

Ausubel, D., R. Montemayor, and P. Svajian. (1977). *Theory of Problems of Adolescent Development*. New York: Grune & Stratton.

Bandura, A., and R.H. Walters. (1959). *Adolescent Aggression*. New York: Ronald Press.

Baric, L., C. MacArthur, and C. Fischer. (1976). 'Norms, Attitudes, and Smoking Behaviour amongst Manchester Students.' *Health Education Journal* 35: 142–50.

Barreca, R. (1991). *They Used to Call Me Snow White ... But I Drifted: Women's Strategic Use of Humor*. Harmondsworth, Eng.: Penguin.

Barthes, R. (1957). *Mythologies*. Paris: Seuil.

Baruch, D.W. (1953). *How to Live with Your Teenager*. New York: McGraw-Hill.

Bauman, Z. (1992). *Intimations of Postmodernity*. London: Routledge.

Berger, A.A. (1984). *Signs in Contemporary Culture: An Introduction to Semiotics*. Salem: Sheffield.

Bergin, T.G., and M. Fisch. (1984). *The New Science of Giambattista Vico*. Ithaca, NY: Cornell University Press.

Britton, J. (1970). *Language and Learning*. Harmondsworth, Eng.: Penguin.

Bruch, H. (1978). *The Golden Cage: The Enigma of Anorexia Nervosa*. Cambridge, Mass.: Harvard University Press.

Brumberg, J.J. (1988). *Fasting Girls: The Emergence of Anorexia Nervosa as a Modern Disease*. Cambridge, Mass.: Harvard University Press.

Bruner, J.S. (1986). *Actual Minds, Possible Worlds*. Cambridge, Mass.: Harvard University Press.

– (1990). *Acts of Meaning*. Cambridge, Mass.: Harvard University Press.

Bühler, K. (1934). *Sprachtheorie: Die Darstellungsfunktion der Sprache*. Jena: Fischer.

Buis, J.M., and D.N. Thompson. (1989). 'Imaginary Audience and Personal Fable: A Brief Review.' *Adolescence* 24: 773–81.

Burke, D. (1991). *Street Talk–1*. Los Angeles: Optima.

– (1992). *Street Talk–2*. Los Angeles: Optima.

Cameron, D. (1992). 'Naming of Parts: Gender, Culture, and Terms for the Penis among American College Students.' *American Speech* 67: 367–82.

Chassin, B., E.H. Roosmalen, and S.A. McDaniel. (1992). 'Adolescent Smoking Intentions: Gender Differences in Peer Context.' *Adolescence* 27: 87–105.

Coleman, J.C., and L. Hendry. (1990). *The Nature of Adolescence*. London: Routledge.

Cooper, D., and L. Anderson-Inman. (1988). 'Language and Socialization.' In *Later Language Development*, ed. M. Nippold, 225–45. Boston: Little, Brown.

Coupland, D. (1991). *Generation X*. New York: St Martin's.

Crook, M. (1991). *The Body Image Trap*. Vancouver: Self-Counsel Press.

Danesi, M. (1988). 'Pubilect: Observations on North American Teenager Talk.' In *The Fourteenth LACUS Forum*, ed. S. Embleton, 433–41. Lake Bluff, Ill.: LACUS.

– (1989a). 'Adolescent Language as Affectively Coded Behavior: Findings of an Observational Research Project.' *Adolescence* 24: 311–20.

– (1989b). 'The Role of Metaphor in Cognition.' *Semiotica* 77: 521–31.

– (1993). 'Smoking Behavior in Adolescence as Signifying Osmosis.' *Semiotica* 96: 53–69.

Dawkins, R. (1976). *The Selfish Gene*. Oxford: Oxford University Press.

– (1987). *The Blind Watchmaker*. Harlow: Longmans.

De Paoli, M. (1988). *Il linguaggio del rock italiano*. Ravenna: Longo.

Desjarlais, L., and J. Rackauskas. (1986). *Adolescent Development*. Toronto: Ontario Ministry of Education.

Di Pietro, R.J. (1973). Review of *Giambattista Vico: An International Symposium*, ed. G. Tagliacozzo and H.V. White, *Foundations of Language* 9: 410–21.

– (1987). *Strategic Interaction*. Cambridge: Cambridge University Press.

Doherty, T. (1988). *Teenagers and Teenpics*. London: Unwin Hyman.

Duncan, B. (1988). *Mass Media and Popular Culture*. Toronto: Harcourt Brace Jovanovich.

Dunphy, D.C. (1963). 'The Social Structure of Urban Adolescent Peer Groups.' *Sociometry* 26: 230–46.

Eble, C.C. (1989). *College Slang 101*. Georgetown, Conn.: Spectacle Lane Press.

Eckert, P. (1988). 'Adolescent Social Structure and the Spread of Linguistic Change.' *Language in Society* 17: 183–207.

Eder, D. (1990). 'Serious and Playful Disputes: Variation on Conflict Talk Among Female Adolescents.' In *Conflict Talk*, ed. D. Grimshaw, 67–84. Cambridge: Cambridge University Press.

Eicher, J.B. (1991). 'Adolescent Dress: A Qualitative Study of Suburban High School Students.' *Adolescence* 26: 680–6.

Ekman, P. (1982). 'Methods for Measuring Facial Action.' In *Handbook of Methods in Nonverbal Behavior*, ed. K.R. Scherer and P. Ekman, 45–90. Cambridge: Cambridge University Press.

Elkind, D. (1967). 'Egocentrism in Adolescence.' *Child Development* 38: 1025–34.

– (1971). *A Sympathetic Understanding of the Child Six to Sixteen.* Boston: Allyn and Bacon.

– (1984). *All Grown Up and No Place to Go.* Reading, Mass.: Addison-Wesley.

– (1988). *The Hurried Child: Growing Up Too Fast Too Soon.* Reading, Mass.: Addison-Wesley.

Engen, T. (1982). *The Perception of Odours.* New York: Academic.

Erikson, E.H. (1950). *Childhood and Society.* New York: Norton.

– (1968). *Identity: Youth and Crisis.* New York: Norton.

Esman, A.H. (1990). *Adolescence and Culture.* New York: Columbia University Press.

Ewen, S. (1988). *All Consuming Images.* New York: Basic.

Firth, J.R. (1951). *Papers in Linguistics, 1934–1951.* Oxford: Oxford University Press.

Fisher, H.E. (1992). *Anatomy of Love.* New York: Norton.

Flay, B.R., J.R. D'Avernas, J.A. Best, M. Kersell, and K. Ryan. (1982). 'Why Young People Smoke and Ways of Preventing Them.' In *Pediatric and Adolescent Behavioral Medicine*, ed. P. Firestone and P. McGrath, 34–53. New York: Springer.

Friedman, L.S., E. Lichtenstein, and A. Biglan. (1985). 'Smoking Onset among Teens: An Empirical Analysis of Initial Situations.' *Addictive Behaviors* 10: 1–13.

Gardner, H. (1982). *Developmental Psychology.* Boston: Little, Brown.

Gendlin, E.T. (1991). 'Thinking beyond Patterns: Body, Language, Situations.' In *The Presence of Feeling in Thought*, ed. B. den Ouden and M. Moen, 22–152. New York: Peter Lang.

Glass, L. (1992). *He Says, She Says: Closing the Communication Gap between the Sexes.* New York: G.P. Putnam's Sons.

Goffman, E. (1959). *The Presentation of Self in Everyday Life*. Garden City, New Jersey: Doubleday.

– (1978). 'Response Cries.' *Language* 54: 787–815.

Goodwin, A. (1992). *Dancing in the Distraction Factory: Music Television and Popular Culture*. Minneapolis: University of Minnesota Press.

Goodwin, C. and A. Duranti. (1992). 'Rethinking Context: An Introduction.' In *Rethinking Context: Language as an Interactive Phenomenon*, ed. A. Duranti and C. Goodwin, 1–13. Cambridge: Cambridge University Press.

Goodwin, C. and M.H. Goodwin. (1992). 'Assessments and the Construction of Context.' In *Rethinking Context: Language as an Interactive Phenomenon*, ed. A. Duranti and C. Goodwin, 34–45. Cambridge: Cambridge University Press.

Gould, S.J. (1977). *Ontogeny and Phylogeny*. Cambridge, Mass.: Harvard University Press.

Green, D.E. (1979). *Teenage Smoking: Immediate and Long Term Patterns*. Washington, DC: Department of Health, Education, and Welfare.

Greenwald, T. (1992). *Rock & Roll*. New York: Friedman.

Grossberg, L. (1992). *We Gotta Get Out of This Place: Popular Conservatism and Postmodern Culture*. London: Routledge.

Gusdorf, G. (1965). *Speaking*. Evanston, Ill.: Northwestern University Press.

Hall, E.T. (1966). *The Hidden Dimension*. New York: Doubleday.

Hall, R.A. (1963). *Idealism in Romance Linguistics*. Ithaca, NY: Cornell University Press.

Hall, S.G. (1904). *Adolescence*. New York: Appleton-Century-Crofts.

Halliday, M.A.K. (1975). *Learning How to Mean: Explorations in the Development of Language*. London: Arnold.

– (1985). *Introduction to Functional Grammar*. London: Arnold.

Hebdige, D. (1979). *Subculture: The Meaning of Style*. London: Routledge.

Hechinger, G., and F.M. Hechinger. (1963). *The Teen-age Tyranny*. New York: Morrow.

Hodge, R., and G. Kress. (1988). *Social Semiotics*. Ithaca, NY: Cornell University Press.

Hoffman, R.R. (1983). 'Recent Research on Metaphor.' *Semiotic Inquiry* 3: 35–61.

Hollander, A. (1988). *Seeing through Clothes*. Harmondsworth, Eng.: Penguin.

Hudson, R. (1984). *Invitation to Linguistics*. Oxford: Robinson.

Hughes, G. (1991). *Swearing*. London: Blackwell.

Hutchison, M. (1990). *The Anatomy of Sex and Power: An Investigation of Mind-Body Politics*. New York: Morrow.

Hymes, D. (1972). 'Models in the Interaction of Language and Social Life.' In *Directions in Sociolinguistics: The Ethnography of Communication*, ed. J. Gumperz and D. Hymes, 45–59. New York: Holt, Rinehart & Winston.

Immelmann, K., and C. Beer. (1989). *A Dictionary of Ethology*. Cambridge, Mass.: Harvard University Press.

Jackson, L.A. (1992). *Physical Appearance and Gender: Sociobiological and Sociocultural Perspectives*. Albany: State University Of New York Press.

Jakobson, R. (1960). 'Linguistics and Poetics.' In *Style and Language*, ed. T. Sebeok, 34–59. Cambridge, Mass.: MIT Press.

Jenni, M.A. (1976). 'Sex Differences in Carrying Behavior.' *Perceptual and Motor Skills* 43: 323–30.

Johnson, M. (1987). *The Body in the Mind: The Bodily Basis of Meaning, Imagination and Reason*. Chicago: University of Chicago Press.

– (1991). 'The Emergence of Meaning in Bodily Experience.' In *The Presence of Feeling in Thought*, ed. B. den Ouden and M. Moen, 153–67. New York: Peter Lang.

Joos, M. (1967). *The Five Clocks*. New York: Harcourt, Brace and World.

Jung, C.G. (1921). *Psychological Types*. New York: Harcourt.

Kannas, L. (1985). 'The Image of Smoking and Non-smoking Young Persons.' *Health Education Journal* 44: 26–30.

Keesing, R.M. (1981). *Cultural Anthropology*. New York: Holt, Rinehart and Winston.

Key, W.B. (1989). *The Age of Manipulation*. New York: Henry Holt.

Klapp, O.E. (1969). *The Collective Search for Identity*. New York: Holt, Rinehart and Winston.

Kniskern, J., A. Biglan, E. Lichtenstein, D. Ary, and L. Bavry. (1983). 'Peer Modeling Effects in the Smoking Behavior of Teenagers.' *Addictive Behaviors* 8: 129–32.

Kohlberg, L. (1969). 'Stage and Sequence: The Cognitive-Developmental Approach to Socialization.' In *Handbook of Socialization Theory and Research*, ed. D.A. Goslin, 345–87. New York: Rand McNally.

– (1978). 'From Is to Ought: How to Commit the Naturalistic Fallacy and Get away with it in the Study of Moral Development.' In *Cognitive Development and Epistemology*, ed. T. Mischel, 83–8. San Francisco: Jossey-Bass.

Kövecses, Z. (1986). *Metaphors of Anger, Pride, and Love: A Lexical Approach to the Structure of Concepts*. Amsterdam: Benjamins.

– (1988). *The Language of Love: The Semantics of Passion in Conversational English*. London: Associated University Presses.

– (1990). *Emotion Concepts*. New York: Springer.

Krosnick, J.A., and C.M. Judd. (1982). 'Transitions in Social Influence of Adolescence: Who Induces Cigarette Smoking?' *Developmental Psychology* 18: 359–68.

Labov, T. (1992). 'Social Language Boundaries among Adolescents.' *American Speech* 67: 339–66.

Labov, W. (1972). *Language in the Inner City*. Philadelphia: University of Pennsylvania Press.

– (1982). 'Social Structure and Peer Terminology in a Black Adolescent Gang.' *Language in Society* 11: 391–413.

Lakoff, G. (1987). *Women, Fire, and Dangerous Things: What Categories Reveal about the Mind*. Chicago: University of Chicago Press.

Lakoff, G., and M. Johnson. (1980). *Metaphors We Live By*. Chicago: University of Chicago Press.

Landau, T. (1989). *About Faces: The Evolution of the Human Face*. New York: Anchor.

Landis, P. (1955). *Understanding Teenagers*. New York: Appleton-Century-Crofts.

Langer, S.K. (1948). *Philosophy in a New Key*. New York: Mentor Books.

Lenski, G.E. (1966). *Power and Privilege: A Theory of Social Stratification*. New York: McGraw-Hill.

Leona, M.H. (1978). 'An Examination of Adolescent Clique Language in a Suburban Secondary School.' *Adolescence* 13: 495–502.

Liebert, R.M. and J.M. Sprafkin. (1988). *The Early Window: Effects of Television on Children and Youth*. New York: Pergamon.

Lynd, R.S. and H.M. Lynd. (1929). *Middletown: A Study in Modern American Culture*. New York: Harcourt, Brace and World.

Malinowski, B. (1923). 'The Problem of Meaning in Primitive Languages.' In *The Meaning of Meaning*, ed. C.K. Ogden and I.A. Richards, 231–45. New York: Harcourt, Brace and World.

Maltz, D., and R. Borker. (1982). 'A Cultural Approach to Male-Female Communication.' In *Language and Social Identity*, ed. J. Gumperz, 196–216. Cambridge: Cambridge University Press.

Manley, R.S. (1989). 'Anorexia and Bulimia Nervosa: Psychological Features, Assessment, and Treatment.' *B.C. Medical Journal* 31: 151–4.

Marshall, P. (1992). *Now I Know Why Tigers Eat Their Young: How to Survive Your Teenagers with Humour*. Vancouver: Whitecap Books.

McDonald, G.W. (1977). 'Parental Identification by the Adolescent: Social Power Approach.' *Journal of Marriage and the Family* 39: 705–19.

McLuhan, M. (1962). *The Gutenberg Galaxy*. Toronto: University of Toronto Press.

– (1964). *Understanding Media*. London: Routledge & Kegan Paul.

Mead, M. (1939). *From the South Seas: Studies of Adolescence and Sex in Primitive Societies*. New York: Morrow.

– (1950). *Coming of Age in Samoa*. New York: New American Library.

Meyer-Eppler, W. (1959). *Grundlagen und Anwendungen der Informationstheorie*. Berlin: Springer Verlag.

Milner, R. (1990). *The Encyclopedia of Evolution: Humanity's Search for Its Origins*. New York: Facts on File.

Milroy, L. (1980). *Language and Social Networks*. Oxford: Blackwell.

Money, J. (1986). *Lovemaps: Clinical Concepts of Sexual/Erotic Health and Pathology, Paraphilia, and Gender Identity from Conception to Maturity*. Baltimore: Johns Hopkins.

Morris, D. (1990). *Animalwatching*. London: Jonathan Cape.

Munro, P. (1989). *Slang U*. New York: Harmony.

Nippold, M.A., ed. (1988). *Later Language Development: Ages Nine through Nineteen*. Boston: Little, Brown.

Nuessel, F. (1991). 'Metaphor and Cognition: A Survey of Recent Publications.' *Journal of Literary Semantics* 20: 37–52.

Ogden, C.K. and I.A. Richards. (1923). *The Meaning of Meaning*. London: Routledge and Kegan Paul.

Okun, M.A. and J.H. Sasfy. (1977). 'Adolescence, the Self-Concept, and Formal Operations.' *Adolescence* 12: 373–9.

Osgood, C.E., G.J. Suci, and P.H. Tannenbaum. (1957). *The Measurement of Meaning*. Urbana: University of Illinois Press.

Pederson, L.L., and N.M. Lefcoe. (1985). 'Cross-sectional Analysis of Variables Related to Cigarette Smoking in Late Adolescence.' *Journal of Drug Education* 13: 305–12.

Peirce, C.S. (1958). *Collected Papers of Charles S. Peirce*. Ed. C. Hartshorne and Paul Weiss. Vol. 1. Cambridge, Mass.: Harvard University Press, 1931–58.

Perry, C.L., J. Killen, L.A. Slinkard, and A.L. McAllister. (1980). 'Peer Teaching and Smoking Prevention among Junior High Students.' *Adolescence* 15: 277–81.

Piaget, J. (1969). *The Child's Conception of the World*. Totowa, NJ: Littlefield, Adams & Co.

Piaget, J., and J. Inhelder. (1969). *The Psychology of the Child*. New York: Basic Books.

Pollio, H., J. Barlow, H. Fine, and M. Pollio. (1977). *The Poetics of Growth: Figurative Language in Psychology, Psychotherapy, and Education*. Hillsdale, NJ: Lawrence Erlbaum Associates.

Rector, M. (1975). *A lenguagem de inventude*. Petrópolis, Brazil: Editora Vozes.

Reek, J. van, M. Drop, and J. Joosten. (1987). 'The Influence of Peers and Parents on the Smoking Behavior of Schoolchildren.' *Journal of School Health* 57: 30–1.

Rice, J.P. (1990). *The Adolescent*. Boston: Allyn and Bacon.

Rizzi, E. (1985). 'Note sul linguaggio dei giovani studenti Bolognesi.' *Rivista Italiana di Dialettologia* 9: 89-102.

Romaine, S. (1984). *The Language of Children and Adolescence*. Oxford: Blackwell.

Ruesch, J. (1972). *Semiotic Approaches to Human Relations*. The Hague: Mouton.

Salinger, J.D. (1951). *The Catcher in the Rye*. Boston: Little, Brown.

– (1953). *Nine Stories*. Boston: Little, Brown.

– (1961). *Franny and Zooey*. Boston: Little, Brown.

– (1963). *Raise High the Roof Beam, Carpenters*. Boston: Little, Brown.

– (1963). *Seymour: An Introduction*. Boston: Little, Brown.

Saussure, F. de (1916). *Cours de linguistique générale*. Paris: Payot.

Schank, R. (1984). *The Cognitive Computer*. Reading, Mass.: Addison-Wesley.

Searle, J.R. (1969). *Speech Acts: An Essay in the Philosophy of Language*. Cambridge: Cambridge University Press.

– (1976). 'A Classification of Illocutionary Acts.' *Language in Society* 5: 1–23.

– (1992). *The Rediscovery of the Mind*. Cambridge, Mass.: MIT Press.

Sebeok, T.A. (1989). 'Fetish.' *American Journal of Semiotics* 6: 51–65.

Shahar, S. (1992). *Childhood in the Middle Ages*. London: Routledge.

Shapiro, T. (1985). 'Adolescent Language: Its Use for Diagnosis, Group Identity, Values, and Treatment.' *Adolescent Psychiatry* 12: 297–311.

Skinner, W.F., J.L. Massey, M. Krohn, and R. Lauer. (1985). 'Social Influences and Constraints on the Initiation and Cessation of Adolescent Tobacco Use.' *Journal of Behavioral Medicine* 8: 353–76.

Slossberg Anderson, E. (1992). *Speaking with Style*. London: Routledge.

Solomon, J. (1988). *The Signs of Our Time*. Los Angeles: Jeremy P. Tarcher.

Steinberg, L. (1987). 'Bound to Bicker.' *Psychology Today* 21: 36–9.

Stern J., and M. Stern. (1992). *Encyclopedia of Pop Culture*. New York: Harper.

Strasburger, V. (1993). *Getting Your Kids to Say 'No' in the '90s When You Said 'Yes' in the Sixties*. New York: Fireside.

Tannen, D. (1990). *You Just Don't Understand: Women and Men in Conversation*. New York: Ballantine.

Thorne, T. (1990). *Dictionary of Contemporary Slang*. London: Bloomsbury.

Titone, R. (1977). 'A Humanistic Approach to Language Behaviour and Language Learning.' *Canadian Modern Language Review* 33: 309–17.

Vestergaard, T., and K. Schrøder. (1985). *The Language of Advertising*. London: Blackwell.

Vine, J. (1970). 'Communication by Facial-Visual Signals.' In *Social Behavior in Birds and Mammals*, ed. J.H. Crook, 279–354. New York: Academic.

Vygotsky, L.S. (1961). *Thought and Language*. Cambridge, Mass.: MIT Press.

– (1984). *Problems of General Psychology. Vol. 2 of Vygotsky's Collected Works*. Ed. and trans. R. Rieber and A. Carton. Cambridge, Mass.: Harvard University Press.

Wallbott, H.G. (1979). 'Gesichtsausdruck: Einführung.' In *Nonverbale Kommunikation*, ed. K.R. Scherer and H.G. Wallbott, 34–45. Weinheim: Beltz.

Whiteley, S. (1992). *The Space between the Notes: Rock and the Counter-Culture*. London: Routledge.

Wicke, P. (1987). *Rock Music: Culture, Aesthetics and Sociology*. Cambridge: Cambridge University Press.

Wittgenstein, L. (1922). *Tractatus Logico-Philosophicus*. London: Routledge and Kegan Paul.

Yates, A. (1989). 'Current Perspectives on the Eating Disorders:

I. History, Psychological, and Biological Aspects.' *Journal of the American Academy of Child Adolescent Psychiatry* 28: 813–28.

– (1990). 'Current Perspectives on the Eating Disorders: II. Treatment, Outcome, and Research Directions.' *Journal of the American Academy of Child Adolescent Psychiatry* 29: 1–9.

# Index